SMUGGLING VILLAGES
of North East Essex

GEORGE PLUCKWELL

IAN HENRY PUBLICATIONS

ISBN 0 86025 403 8

The drawing on the cover is by
W E Borrett

Printed by WBC Print, Bristol

for Ian Henry Publications, Ltd.
20 Park Drive, Romford, Essex RM1 4LH

Rowhedge

Rowhedge, where I have lived for over twenty years in an old fisherman's smuggling cottage, reputedly over 200 years old, is 2½ miles from Colchester, in the parish of East Donyland. A 1909 Essex Guide describes the village as a fishing community on the west bank of the tidal River Colne, with shipyards, maltings and breweries.

The village itself – or at least its land – dates back to Iron Age Britain in about 5 A.D. The ground was then all part of the Iceni fortress of Camulodunum, covering some 12 to 16 square miles, a true fortress city bordered by the Rivers Colne and Roman. It was constructed entirely of wood from the great forests of Essex and was the stronghold of powerful Cunobelin and can be regarded as the capital city of Iron Age Britain.

Cunobelin died abour A.D.41 after a long reign and shortly Claudius annexed England and occupied Camulodunum, setting up a colony in part of the city's grounds that he called Victrix or Victoria, in honour of Victory and Claudiana in honour of himself. He decreed that the Temple of Claudius be built to his deity, thought to be the first brick and stone building erected in Britain.

Camulodunum was destroyed in Boudicca's revolt in A.D.61, while trying to avenge herself and her daughters and, incidentally, to shake off the yoke of Rome. After that the Romans began to wall in their colony, just a part of the ancient city, and this eventually became known as Colchester.

But Rowhedge and the other sections just reverted to farmlands and villas, over a gradual process. When the Romans left these shores about 428, all culture went with them. For the Saxons sailed up the unguarded Colne and, as they hated walls and houses, made camps at Rowhedge, calling the area East Donulanda, which meant hilly.

The Saxons were saints compared with the terrible marauding Danes, who came up the river four hundred years later, sacking and pillaging the whole neighbourhood.

After 910 Edward the Elder came to Colchester with his West Saxon army and drove the Danes out. At this time the town walls were repaired.

Following the Norman Conquest Rowhedge and East Donulanda seems to have been the property of Queen Maud, wife of King Stephen (1105-54). Maud was very keen on religious houses and life and eventually swapped East Dunulanda with the monks of Colchester's St John's Benedictine Abbey, for land in another area. So the district lived contentedly with the monks as Lords of the Manor for many centuries.

The old East Donyland church was built in the Norman era, but was pulled down when the new church was built.

After the Reformation under Henry VIII, East Doniland, as it was by then spelt, was taken by the crown and given, or sold, to three main owners.

Chiefly the lordly de Veres of Castle Heding-ham, who had lands at Rowhedge Reach; Sir Thomas Darcy, who seemed to have owned half Essex at one period; and the Jobsons, Lords of the Manors of East and West Doniland. The Manor House called East Donyland Hall was built for the Jobsons about 1540 and a Georgian front was later added.

Sir Francis Jobson got rich mostly from the spoils of the local abbeys and also had a Manor House at West Doniland (now known as Berechurch), besides numerous other lands and titles.

Rev. Benton, vicar of the adjacent parish of Fingringhoe, wrote at length about Rowhedge Old Church for the Archaeological Society, pointing out that the old graveyard is still there, up past the Recreation Ground by the Fingringhoe Road. In by-gone days that housed the entire village and was also a kind of open heath, whence come Heath House and, later, Heath Road. The churchyard was still used for burials in the 1930s, but there is hardly anything left to indicate the demolished church.

Rev. J M Easterling was rector of Rowhedge from 1900 to 1929 and had located a picture of the former church, but the parish chest does not contain one scrap of paper referring either to the demolition of the ancient St Laurence or the erection of its successor. M Benton has discovered a pen and ink sketch in the Probert Collection of drawings of Essex churches in the Archaeological Library. This was dated 1 October, 1801; although unsigned there is evidence to show that the artist was a Captain Sanders of Colchester.

The sketch shows a single storied structure with a porch and belfry, surrounded by a picket fence and various trees. There was also another picture of the historic font, which is believed to contain the Jobson coat of arms. In 1840 this 15th century font was purchased by Rev F Curtis and installed in St Leonard's Church, Colchester, where it stands to this day, a token of Rowhedge's past. St Leonard's has recently been made redundant, the cost of repairing it being over a quarter of a million pounds: what will have happened to Rowhedge's font?

Morant was brief enough in his monumental *History of Essex* with the story of East Donyland and its venerable church, which he said is of one piece, with the chancel both tyled [tiled] and small; at the west end there is, he said, a little turret containing a bell.

Mr Benton commented, "This hardly does more

The Norman church of East Donyland: painting by V Stone
East Donyland Church, Rowhedge

than Holman (the historian) who wrote fifty years
earlier than Morant, saying the turret is a poor
wooden erection and, like so many churches in Essex,
it was erected in the 12th century and there is no
doubt there was a tower here of sorts, for the church
inventory of 1547 mentions bells in the steppy
[steeple] and it records that in 1633 their steeple
wants bordirige [boarding] on the top and their belfry
doors are rotten." Moreover, it was stated in 1610
that the steple [steeple] of the church was ready to
fall down and no prayers could stop it.

So the tower could hardly have been a stone
building, but probably a timber bell turret resting on
oak framing within the walls of the nave: a type of
belfry common to this part of Essex.

Rev. Benton organised a dig on the old church
site in 1926 and it was discovered that the stone
paving of the nave was still intact. The nave was
approximately 38 by 20 feet, the size of the Norman
nave. The following entry occurs in some old papers,
"Mr T Scott, carpenter, informs me that Donyland
Old Church was purchased by Mr Jenkins, builder, for
the sum of between £50 and £60 in 1844." The reason
for its abandonment and destruction was that it was
too far out of the village which had then developed
around the River Colne area, which is where the
majority of the 700 parishioners reside. Further, the
church provided insufficient accommodation and was
incapable of enlargement.

The new St Laurence was built by William
Mason of Ipswich in 1838 a mile and a half nearer
Rowhedge village at a cost of £2,000. The *Essex
County Standard* said, "This structure calls for little
remark. Of white brick and octagonal in shape it is
an imitation of the Chapter House of York Minster."
The oak pews are set in such a way that one can see
the minister at all times. The population in 1863 was
1,053.

In 1777 John Chapman's map of Essex shows

Row-Hedge with rows of trees or hedges by the River Colne and with the old parsonage way down the riverside High Street, miles away from the Saxon and Norman church. A map of 1808 shows Donyland Heath and the terrace of cottages in Head Street, but no main Rowhedge Road to Colchester. The main road was probably the Fingringhoe road which still goes by the Ipswich Arms at the top of the village.

Further glimpses into the history of the old church are given in a list of church goods that Rev. Benton probably got from the ancient Church Chest. A new pulpit was provided by the Churchwardens in 1547 - "Paide out unto the carpynter for making of the pulpyt and the pale of the Churchyarde. A further sum was spent on garnetts and nayles for ye pulpyt."

A casual reference to the seating in the church in the early 17th century occurs in a minute book of the Archdeaconary. In 1615 William Ball was presented to the Church Court of Colchester for not sitting in the stole [stalls]. He was admonished to sit by Mr Archdeacon. He pleaded that the seat is so full he could not sit there. Ball was ordered to apologise publicly on a Sunday for contempt of court. He apologised and carried out his penance on 3rd July, 1616, and the necessary certificate was given by the Church Court to show he had paid in full for his sins. Fines amounting to 12 pence were also discharged.

In 1707 the bell was cracked and was ordered to be new run (repaired). Possibly this was the same bell which, according to Rev Easterling of Rowhedge, had been stolen from the old church in about 1834 and was supposed to have been sunk in the Mill Pond at Fingringhoe and then taken away by crooks to the West of England - bells were valuable items. This information was given to the rector by an old Rowhedger, a clerk, who remembered being told the story.

The altar vessels were renewed in the first years of Queen Victoria's reign.

During Edward VI's short reign there was a 'chalis of sylver, one coverplate, a clothe for the challis and one to hang over the roods: a candlestick and a latten [lantern] and 2 bellys [bells] in the steppie [steeple].' In 1634 the church possessed a small chalice of silver and a flagon of pewter, the former vessel may have been the cup purchased in Elizabeth I's time to replace the medieval chalice left by Edward VI's commissioners.

Early registers are missing and the present book begins in 1731. William Kyrbye, rector of East Donyland, was always getting himself into hot water. In 1579 he was accused by Master Maystone's wife, before the Church Court, that he was a common alehouse haunter and frequenter of a harlot's house. Sex and drink appear to have been his failings and, in 1581, he again appeared before an Archdeaconary Court charged by a woman parishioner 'that the Church at East Doniland is often closed and sometimes we haith ne services at all'. The outcome of this serious charge is unknown, but it is a fair bet that W Kyrbye must have been unfrocked sooner or later: he seems to have been a most unsuitable pastor.

Rev. Benton tells a strange story of the two brasses. It seems they were taken from the floor of the old church and placed underneath a table in the new St Laurence building and then forgotten for many years. Later they were framed in oak and hung on the new church walls as proof of our rich history. They were originally attached to the stone slab tombs on the floor of the old church. The first brass represents Mary Gray, wife of the Lord of the Manor, Edward Jobson: her standing effigy is 20½ inches high. She wears a large hood which falls down the back, nearly to the ground. She has a neck ruff of the period and a plain gown. The inscription plate, nearly 18 by 4½ inches, records that she was the wife of William Gray, Esq., and formerly married to Edward

Jobson and Nicholas Marshall "and with alachrytee of
spirit she surrendered her soule unto ye hands of her
redeemer about ye middle of July 1627 aged 56". The
pedigree of Mary Gray is confused and contradictory.
The lady was apparently a daughter of John Bode of
Rochford and his wife, Joan, daughter and heiress of
Edward Strangeman. She appears to have had four
husbands; firstly Thomas Collings, then Nicholas
Marshall, thirdly Edward Jobson (who died without
male issue on 28th May, 1590) and, lastly, William
Gray, whom she wed in February, 1598. So the Manor
of East Doniland and its Hall passed into the Gray
family.

The second brass is of her son, Nicholas
Marshall, by her second spouse. It is the same height
as his mother's and the figure is shown standing in
an attitude of prayer with a half turn to the right.
He is depicted with long hair and beard and
moustache. He wears a large neck ruffle, doublet,
stuffed breeches and hose. His garters and shoes are
tied with bows and a rapier hangs at his left side,
while over all is a short, open cloak. The figure of a
child at his left foot is lost (said Holman, the
Historian). The inscription, on a separate plate, states
that he was of Benyngham, Suffolk, and the son of
Mary Gray. He married, first, Elizabeth, daughter of
Sir John Browne, knight, of Flamberts, Cold Norton.
His second wife was Alice, daughter of G Brooke,
Esq., of Aspall, Suffolk. He died in 1621 aged 36 and
was survived by Alice.

Why Elizabeth Marshall, first wife of Nicholas,
got such a magnificent monument, while her successor
only got a brass will never be known, but her fine
monument in alabaster was taken from the old church
and installed in the new building. It shows her seated
effigy, which has withstood the stress of the
centuries so well that the only sign of damage is a
mutilated hand. It is dated 1613 and has a long
epitaph which reads: "In Heaven her Soule, on Earth

her corpse is inclosed".

There are tablets to the Haven family, Lords of East Donyland Manor in the Victorian period: Philip, who died in 1874, and others from 1816 to 1856, which were probably transferred from the old church, although it is believed that the Havens had a family vault underneath the old church until 1837.

Another later memorial is to William Harecourt Torricano, who died in 1828, having been a civil servant with the Madras establishment of the Honourable East India Company for 43 years. One of his relations, perhaps his son, was rector of Rowhedge for a number of years, for in *Kelly's Directory* there is mention of the Rev. Vicessimus Torricano as incumbent. He helped to raise the money for the new St Laurence's.

It is sad to wake up one morning and find that nearly all the old characters of a village have disappeared. Like Miss Curle, the old cat lady; Miss Jones, the wonderful Swan poetess; and even the colourful old Dutch lady. All now, alas, gone into the pages of village history.

But the remaining Rowhedge pubs, like the Anchor, the Albion, and the Freemasons, still have a marvellous atmosphere of sailing boats, smugglers and river yarns rich in Essex heritage. In times gone by there were 16 pubs in Rowhedge - more pubs, almost, that cottages! Perhaps the floating population on the river let these places thrive.

There is the former Royal Oak Tree inn, now converted to a home as The Oaks, up Rectory Road. There is also the single storey beer house called The Cherry Tree, up Taylors Road, now transformed into a desireable bungalow with more rooms added. The Three Crowns in Head Street closed fairly recently: twenty years ago it was managed by Mr Wisby. A Tudor construction of heavy beams and plaster, it was one of the oldest buildings in the area, full of low

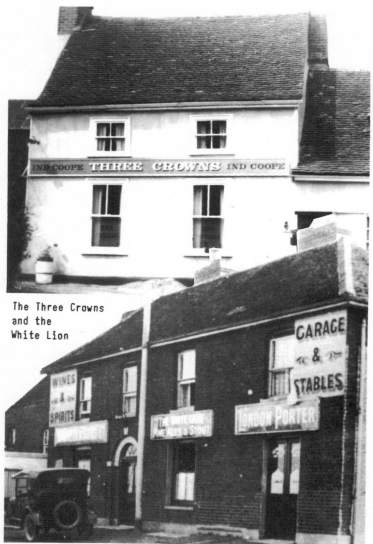

The Three Crowns
and the
White Lion

beamed ceilings with horse brasses, oil lamps and old fashioned hand counter pumps. Mr Wisby, red cheeked and talkative, was the ideal country landlord and one could, in fine weather, enjoy a beer outside on the gravel forecourt, relaxing at tressel tables and contemplating the life of the High Street.

The White Lion, opposite Lion Quay, had a passage and a funny little window with a sliding flap where drinks were ordered for various bars. Once it had been a captains' drinking place of merit. The outside cellar flaps have long since gone and the pub has been made into two charming houses with raised dormer windows in the rear slanting at an attractive angle under the cobble tile roof.

The Anchor still sits almost astride the bank of the River Colne and is an interesting gem of character. There is a collection of bottles on the top shelves behind the bar counter and a big framed picture of an old fisherman who recalls 'The Ancient Mariner'. In the back area of the public bar the old ship's mast supporting the ceiling should be noted.

Former landlord, John Wilkinshaw and his wife, Shirley, had been at the Anchor for many years. In the summer one can sit outside at round tables shaded by colourful umbrellas and watch, if the tide is right, the river life go by: cargo boats travelling back and forth to Colchester quay, private motor boats, sailing dinghies, and even a few fishing boats making their way to the North Sea.

The Albion, another smuggling inn of true character, is further down the High Street, facing the tidal river, and has been turned into a comfortable, lively place. It still has the historic beam where the Redcoat captain was barbarically hung by the Row-hedge smuggling team for seeing too much: one can see the iron hook to this very day. The unfortunate captain's ghost is said to haunt this place and has been seen on occasions. Mrs Willoughby told me of the time her brother saw it walking up Albion Street, dressed in 18th century costume like something from Nelson's heyday.

Of local smuggling stories one relates how a rough, tough bunch of Rowhedge villains marched on the Customs shed and warehouse at Colchester to steal their impounded tea, confiscated a few days previously by the Officers. They broke down the warehouse doors and loaded the chests of tea on to their carts, all the local people being too nervous to stop the rogues.

The Albion had cellars stretching almost under the river bank and would have been a very useful inn for the smuggling trade. There was a small trap-door behind the bar which led up from the vast underground cellars, which were probably used to hide illegal cargo - rum, gin, whisky.

Further down the High Street, the former Ship Inn was, without doubt, the biggest hostelry in the village. A high, looming building with numerous attics, much renovated today. Some twenty years ago the Ship had been made into a pair of houses lived in and owned by Miss Curle, the old cat lady, whose father owned nearly half the surrounding village at one time.

Miss Curle, benefactor to countless felines, who wrote children's stories and poems, illustrated with her wonderful, clever cat, mouse and bird drawings. She had a tragic life, for her strict Victorian papa had locked her in a big cupboard because she wished to marry a dashing Army officer, of whom her father did not approve; so she devoted her life to caring for stray cats and did a grand job.

The Ship Inn was riddled with secret passages that led down to the waterside and other houses, and had little spy windows built up on the side of the inn, used by those cunning smugglers to send candle-light messages at night when all was quiet in the village and they wanted to move the booty, while keeping a wary eye open for the Customs men.

An enjoyable walk is along to the Freemasons'

Arms, going up twisting Church Street, past the wooden sailing lofts and sea captains' back gardens, with their masts that support the washing lines, causing the clothes to be strung high to dance over the rooftops.

The Freemasons nestles almost on top of St Laurence's Church and is a very quaint place, appearing from the front to be like a Victorian ale-house with a low doorway and sashcord windows, but the back section is high and lofty. Mine hosts are John and Jill Vallis who have made the Freemasons' warm and inviting and full of river and boating people, besides golfers and local footballers. There is an unusual painting on the wall done by a German prisoner of war of people winkling at Fingringhoe or Mersea.

John has a special Lifeboat and Harvest Festival once a year and the bars ring with goods being auctioned off; you can sup your pint and rub shoulders with the local celebrities and hear the organ playing 'Bringing in the Sheaves' in true country fashion.

Mention must be made of Joe Percival of the Ipswich Arms. He and his beer house had character such as will never be seen in these modern plastic mock-Tudor inns that are flooding our countryside. Joe's inn was on the outskirts of the village, about a mile's walk up Rectory Road. It was a low slanting building that touched the ground at the back in true Essex style - at least the sloping roof did. It faced the Woods (War Office property) and was on the small crossroads in open far-flung farmland. Today much has changed, for Joe has retired and departed to the comfortable confines of an almshouse in Colchester, but to enter Joe's was like stepping into the time of our forefathers. He never held a spirit licence, so sold beer and wines. His saloon, or best parlour, was crowded with carpet covered Victorian sofas and chairs. Stuffed birds looked at you from

The Ipswich Arms, c. 1900. Now called "Walnut Tree"

within their glass cases and a stale beer odour
reminded you of where you were sitting. Joe was very
proud of his spacious public bar with photos and
prints of his family and of sailing ships. His father
once served as a steward on the Royal Yacht *Britan-
ia*, when King Teddy was on the throne.

Joe had some interesting paintings on the walls,
executed by prisoners of war. One showed an old man
eaten up with gout called, appropriately enough,
'Gouty Corner'. Another was of an Essex fisherman
peeping through a hole in the fence at a lovely young
woman (like a seaside postcard). Joe Percival had
been at the pub for over 40 years and was to become
a local legend in his own lifetime.

He led a Robinson Crusoe existence, growing
his own vegetables, catching wild rabbits for the pot
and cooking everything in his pressure cooker. Joe
only biked to Rowhedge Post Office once a week to
collect his pension and get other needed supplies.

Two undesireable blokes tried to rob Joe one
dark and dismal night. They attempted to break into
the rather isolated Ipswich Arms, but Joe proved to
be their match, appearing at a front bedroom window
brandishing a shot gun in western fashion. They
scooted like frightened rabbits and were later caught
for doing other jobs in the district.

You never asked Joe for the drink you required
because, towards the end of his long innings, he let
his stocks get low, so it was a case of saying, "Have
you got a stout, please, Joe, or a drop of sherry?"

He often related tales of old Rowhedge. For
instance he said that in the 18th century a sailing
race was organised for Essex fishing smacks. Captain
Hopkins of Wivenhoe organised one event for Rowhedge, Wivenhoe, Brightlingsea and Mersea boats. They
raced for a grand silver cup, which was won by
Captain Cook of Rowhedge.

In that same period a 17 ton ship smuggled and
fished at Rowhedge, called *The Prince of Orange*.

A village is a place where nothing seems to happen, but everything happens on the quiet. Even smuggling.

In the tough old days there were the pirates who captured and plundered ships on the high seas. The wreckers altered navigation warning lights so that many a trim vessel went aground thus giving the wreckers the chance to claim both cargo and boat as salvage. Then there were the smugglers, who often worked for a large ring, with some educated local dignitary in the top position - the brains behind the outfit, so to speak. They smuggled goods in and out of the country trying to deceive the Customs and not pay the required duty.

Some men did one of the above; others indulged in all three.

It must have been like a quayside scene from Robert Louis Stevenson's *Treasure Island* at Rowhedge at that period. The ancient inns full of swaggering seafaring captains, some perhaps with wooden legs and parrots perched on their shoulders. The tall masts of the numerous sailing ships moored alongside the Rowhedge river bank would give the village a proper nautical flavour.

Perhaps there were many Jim Hawkins about as cabin-boys on the long sailing ships and schooners that ploughed the seas. Sails along the River Colne at high tide would prove there was plenty of treasure and wine to be had for the picking.

It was estimated that three million pounds of tea was smuggled into England each year, besides tobacco, brandy and silk from the continent. Some of the bosses became very wealthy. A pound of tea costing 7d [about 3p] in Holland could be sold in England for twenty-four shillings [£1.20].

But if the profits were sky high, the men had to take risks, although gold will always be before men's eyes like the donkey and the carrot. Excise men were hoodwinked and driven away by Rowhedge villagers; local officers were bribed to stay out of sight when a run was made and few people would assist the Customs Officers because the artful smugglers had agents everywhere and soon sought a terrible revenge if 'shopped' by an informer.

Apart from the public houses, there is a dark lane of tree leading down from the Battleswick Farm in Rowhedge Lane to the Colneside: another ideal location for smugglers under the cover of a black night to drive their packhorses laden with contraband to the farmhouse that doubtless had secret hidey holes in the barns and cellars.

Ghost stories were spread about by the smugglers to keep people indoors and to account for the strange noises heard at night when they were moving their stuff. Even tombs in the old churchyard were used to store the precious booty, while another favourite place was the church tower.

The Mariners' Chapel, down Chapel Street, was also used by the smuggling rascals. It seems they even had a key to the chapel and often stored contraband there, keeping barrels underneath the oak pews and high in the roof loft. One Sunday, as Customs and Excise men searched the village for illegal cargo, the fishing families who made up the Mariners' congregation sang loudly, not knowing there was a store of smuggled spirits over their heads in the leaning chapel loft.

When walking across the little donkey path to neighbouring Fingringhoe one can see the Roman River glittering through a belt of trees going towards the Mill. That is a smuggling location if ever there was one, the trees and river so handy for sailing boats to slip up from the Colne and the little dinghies to row silently ashore, to where waiting gangs could transport the illict booty to the old Whalebone Inn. This is an inn near Fingringhoe Green by the big oak tree that is hundreds of years old.

Across the Colne Wivenhoe can be seen,

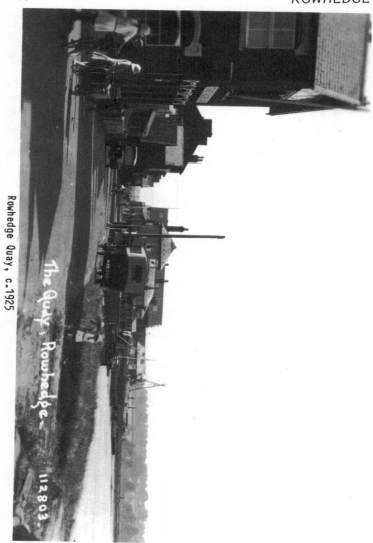

Rowhedge Quay, c.1925

another Colneside village of hearty smuggling tales
and atmosphere. There is an old quayside with houses
of all periods and architecture jumbled together, a
mixture of colourwash plaster and weatherboarded
sailing lofts. The church tower of St Mary the Virgin,
with its crowning cupola must have been a good look-
out station for the 'rum ol' boys' of years ago.

There was a Customs man who dwelt here and
whose name became something of a legend: Daniel
Harvey is supposed to have caught more smugglers
that he had hot dinners and his appearance was said
to put the fear of God into any Customs-hoodwinking
knaves.

The Three Crowns near Shipyard Corner once
had a lightning Customs raid and the quick-thinking
landlady hid a tub of rum underneath her long skirts,
the artful old dame!

And all around are other similar villages.
Peldon, where they reputedly hid smuggled goods in
the duck pond. Mersea Island, where the wreckers
changed the warning lights luring many ships to their
destruction on the treacherous sandbanks, while the
cheeky natives rowed out offering to save the
drowning crews and salvaging the wrecks.

A cult has grown up that contrabandists, like
highwaymen, were romantic. Well, perhaps some had
an eye for the innkeeper's lovely daughter with eyes
as black as ebony, but most were ordinary fishermen
who lived their daily lives working the rivers and the
North Sea for their families. Contraband was a side-
line occupation for them, although the extra money
was always welcome. However, some squires lived like
lords and had their country houses transformed into
minor palaces on the proceeds of being the big noises
behind the smuggling or, as they referred to it, 'the
trade'.

In the 18th century smuggling grew to an
alarming degree and the local gangs were running
cargoes through the countryside and forever

challenging the Revenue men. Large cutters often
brought contraband ashore in the daytime, landing it
on the coast or up the Colne. Some of the smugglers'
ships were big, like Stephen Marsh's 140 ton vessel,
manned by 35 crew and a boy. The Revenue cutters
were tremendous too and the *Repulse* was built at
Colchester in 1778 as one of six owned by Captain
Harvey of Wivenhoe. The dreaded Captain Harvey
hired them to the authorities complete with crew and
often acted as Chief Skipper. The *Repulse*, the terror
of the Rowhedge smugglers, was 210 tons with 16
carriage and 12 swivel guns.

The poor fishermen trying to outwit Harvey and
his men were willing to take the chance of trans-
portation, imprisonment or even death to make a
little money on the side.

Approaching Rowhedge from Colchester centre
you went down the Rowhedge Road, little more than
a lane, and entered the village through Chapel Street,
going over the brook and by the white gate that was
closed at night. Going up Chapel Street, past the
Mariners' Chapel and many older cottages, you
entered High Street past facing rows of cottages.

When a job concerning contraband was being
carried out, mostly at night if the tide was right,
some men would be posted about the village streets
as lookouts, keeping a wary eye open for the Customs
officers who might appear at any moment like a bad
dream. The stuff was quickly unloaded from the
slender sailing ships that could tackle the Colne with
ease on the full tide. The loot was carefully stored in
the cottages, some under the sitting room floor
through a little trap-door concealed by rush matting
or rugs.

Watchers also observed from the tiny spy
windows in the eaves of buildings, waving candles and
lanterns for special signals in their own agreed codes.
Perhaps weeks later the goods would be transported
hidden in wagons to their contacts all over Essex.

Rowhedge High Street, c.1900. Georgian Dark House middle left, followed by Three Crowns inn sign

The ordinary smuggler would be paid in cash or kind on the orders of the kingpin. Free kegs of rum were often shared about the village to buy silence for their secret deeds, while many a weatherbeaten retired skipper puffed contentedly on his pipe of smuggled tobacco.

In Essex the Revenue men were called Gaugers and the contrabandists were known as Owlers. Some old salts named the coastguards affectionately Brass Buttons.

The Darkhouse, down the High Street, on the corner of Darkhouse Lane, facing the River Colne, could tell many a smugglers' tale if only walls could speak. It was built in Georgian times of red brick with an attractive white pillared entrance porch and, to this day, is certainly impressive.

Young Miss Molly lived there with her elderly widowed mother, the former wife of a local sea captain. Miss Molly, lovely, with clear blue eyes like cornflowers and flowing golden hair like buttercups, had a secret lover. The youthful Captain John Pim sailed a trim cutter and also indulged in part-time smuggling or free trade, as they called it.

When a run was being made on a moonless night, Captain Pim would navigate his boat up the Colne, carefully peering through his telescope for Miss Molly's signal. If there were no Customs men about and the coast was clear, she would lift the blind in a front window and light a candle, placing her fat, much-petted black cat, The Bosun, alongside the burning candle on the window-sill. After the contraband had been unloaded and removed to the various hiding places in the village, the captain would kiss his sweetheart and, as the tide waits for no man, depart upriver to Colchester Hythe Port where he would have legal cargo to discharge. The story has a happy ending, for they later married and lived to a great age in that same Darkhouse, still indulging in the odd bit of smuggling on the side.

In Colchester Castle there are some relics of the smuggling days. A lantern made from an old whisky bottle, a case of hydrometers used at the end of the 18th century to test the strength of spirits, a Customs officer's 'barker' or pocket pistol, and a strike-a-light tinder box in the form of a flintlock pistol. An Owler's lantern, round with a pointed top, used on the Essex marshes is there too, besides a wooden spirit keg (alas, empty), a wine muller and brand tongs. All speak silently of that smuggling past long since vanished.

Anti-smuggling laws were often passed by Parliament, but the lowering of taxes was the real deterrent to smuggling. When the profits hit rock-bottom, it wasn't a thriving enterprise any longer.

As a boy Dan King had learnt to swim in the river and, when into his eighties, he knew Rowhedge like the back of his hand. He dwelt in a snug cottage up Albion Street and often told tales of the rich past. On the subject of smuggling, however, he would shut up like a clam and smile, nodding his head. "Well, boy," he would say in broad Essex dialect, "Can't say nothing. You must remember all the villagers were related in those days. It was a close knit community. You wouldn't inform on your relations, now, boy, would you? But I can tell you smuggling went on well into Queen Victoria's reign."

He told of the mock-Tudor almshouses just off Albion Street built by Lord Paget, a yacht racing man, who did a lot of good for the local villagers, besides employing crews to sail his graceful boats, winning many cups and prizes.

Arnold Timer, who went about the village in a navy jersey and a checked cap, selling eggs, vegetables and flowers from his small-holding, told of his grandfather who 'was a North Sea fisherman; sometimes they would be gone for months and have a very small catch. Smuggling stuff helped them

Rowhedge Regatta, 1905

supplement their income, keeping them ticking over, so to speak'.

In the 19th century Rowhedge was full of racing yachts and the local men sought a berth in the spring by seeking out the many local sea captains. The yachts were predominantly crewed by Rowhedgers, each man receiving free yachting clothes supplied by the owners, something like two Guernseys with the boat and owner's name stitched across the chest, two pairs of pilot-cloth trousers, a seaman's cap, a pair of canvas deck shoes and a best pair of black leather shoes. They were also given a suit of oilskins to keep them dry in foul weather.

Captain Jesse Cranfield was at the helm of the racing schooner *Cicely* in 1902. The King's Cup during Cowes Week in 1912 was won by *Cariad*, steered by Captain Barry Smith, another Rowhedger. Captain Jack Carter of Rowhedge skippered the *Royal Britannia* for King George V until 1913.

The *Britannia* was famous as one of the greatest racing craft of the time: built for the Prince of Wales in Glasgow in 1893, she was 123 feet long, with a beam of 23 feet. The mast was 110 feet high and she had a displacement of 221 tons. She raced for more than 40 years, winning 360 prizes, 231 of them firsts, from 615 starts. In later years she was the pride of George V and when he died, in 1936, she was towed out to sea and scuttled: he did not wish her to be sailed by anyone else.

In 1927 Sir William Burton's new yacht *Lyruna* was skippered by Captain James Barnard of Rowhedge and beat all competitors.

Joe Percival told an amusing tale with a local flavour. Captain William Cranfield of the village once competed in a Tollesbury Regatta in the early nineteen hundreds. He sailed the *Sunbeam,* and won the cup. He sailed up the Colne for home, leaving his brother Captain Stephen Cranfield to collect the Cup and bring it to a little celebration to be held at

Rowhedge. They waited for three whole days before Stephen arrived with a terrible hangover. He had been detained, getting wet inside!

Another Cranfield was Lemon, who crewed for Sir Thomas Lipton on the renowned racer *Shamrock V*. Sir Thomas, known as the floating grocer, was the son of a papermill worker, leaving school at the age of 9 and, by hard work and brains, finding room at the top. By the age of 30 he had 8,000 employees and a string of grocery shops all over England. Five times he tried and failed to lift the America's Cup, the jewel of the yachting world. Eventually they gave him a special America's Cup, inscribed 'To the greatest loser in the world'.

He had launched six yachts named *Shamrock* to try to capture that sought-after prize over 32 years and his sailing passion caught the imagination of the nation. He spent over half a milion pounds in his glorious, but fruitless, endeavour - he had more luck with his chain of stores!

The Wonder was a fishing smack sailed by the noted Rowhedge skipper Captain James Carter. His good fortune in fishing with her earned him the proud nickname 'Lucky Wonder'. Unfortunately she sank in 1893 during a homeward voyage loaded with sprats. They shifted and burst her forward bulkhead. *The Wonder*, not to be forgotten or outdone, was eventually raised and made 6 feet bigger by Harris Boatyard of Rowhedge: she lived to catch many more sprats.

The Everard coaster *Sincerity* was grounded between Rowhedge and Hythe in 1936. She unfortunately laid across the channel, causing the river to be blocked for a few tides. Later, the Aldous tug *Bricklesey* and another coaster pulled her clear. The *Sincerity* was built by F T Everard of Yorkshire and carried coal for the Colchester gasworks. A German cargo boat went aground near that same spot recently. It was stuck in the mud for three weeks waiting for a high tide to carry it off: meanwhile the

London Stores, High Street, c.1900. Crow's Nest, 1970

crew would paddle ashore and visit the local pubs.

The *Ellen* was built for Mr Martin, a fisherman of Rowhedge, and later had other owners. She often went spratting in the due season and was known as 'The Little Ellen', to distinguish her from the larger smack owned by Captain Richard Cranfield, which often went stow-boating.   The 50 foot larger *Ellen* was built at Wivenhoe in 1886 for Walter Leavett, who owned the Rowhedge Ferry. He let her to fishermen in the winter and to yachting parties in the summer. She was often let for shrimping and made several journeys to the continent with a Rowhedge crew.

Richard Cranfield bought her for £250 and she paid for herself in 18 months by good skilful fishing by local men. After 40 years with the Rowhedge smack fleet she was sold to Mr Harvey Death of Brightlingsea, who often used her for fishing until the late 30s. Then, sadly, she was hulked.

Near the River Colne end of Regent Street is a curious cottage that appears to be something out of *Alice in Wonderland*. This is owned by Mr Crow, the village grocer, who stores odds and ends there, but this little bungalow has a long history. At the turn of the century it was used for the first Methodist meetings in Rowhedge, although how they crammed into that tiny room cannot be imagined: the present Methodist Church in Regent Street was erected in 1913. Then the little hut became a barber's shop. Then Mr Crow used it for storing merchandise when he leased Crow's Nest, the delightful village stores. Now that has been demolished, but Riverside Motors have used the red Essex bricks for building a smart new wall round the area, so the little cottage stands today proudly boasting its new entrance pillars from Mr Crow's old shop.

Another house with a long history is Quay House, in the High Street. A Georgian facade disguises the big, rambling Tudor section at the rear, timbered with many heavy beams. The Pearson family has lived there for many generations. Mrs Wendy Baiswick (nee Pearson) tells of her great-grandfather, who was a shipwright and who painted the sailing ships' spars and masts in one of the spacious front rooms of Quay House. The Pearsons must have been a family of note in those days as the quay opposite also belonged to them: this is now owned by the Village Council, so anyone can sit by the river enjoying the delights of boats, country air and the panoramic background of Rowhedge.

Rowhedge Ironworks Shipyard deserves a mention. In 1904 Walter Oxton, Frank Ernest Maslen and Lewis Penrose Foster, all then in their thirties and on the staff of Swan Hunter & Wigham Richardson, Ltd., realised their burning ambition to have a yard of their own. By borrowing money from their fathers they purchased Donyland Shipyard, Ltd. and were incorporated as The Rowhedge Ironworks Company, Ltd., on 22 February, 1905. Each of the directors drew the princely sum of £3 a week, Maslen acting as Secretary and Naval Architect, Oxton as the designer of the steam engines built at Rowhedge, and Foster as Works Manager.

The village of Rowhedge had a population of 1,200 and the building of sea-going craft was no new thing to the village community. The earliest record was on a bill of sale dated 29 September, 1770: the customer, a West Mersea oysterman, took delivery on consideration of the sum of £120 of lawful money of Great Britain of all that good hull or vessel called or known by the name *Neptune* of the burthen of 25 tons or thereabouts. The present Rowhedge Shipyard consists of the Upper Yard devoted to building steel ships and constructional steelwork and the Lower Yard which is concerned with building wooden vessels and repairs to all types of craft.

The original nucleus of the Upper Yard was shown in the 1839 Tithe Award Map, which showed a

Harris's Shipyard, c.1914

shipyard in the north of the parish owned by Susannah Cole and occupied by William Cheek. This covered an area of two rods, 14 perches, and the cottage where William Cheek lived is still standing, forming part of the general stores. James Harris first appears as a shipwright in the directory of 1848 and a Mrs Puxley in *Kelly's Directory* of 1886. They were the only other boat-builders in Rowhedge, and James Harris became Harris Brothers, Ltd. Mrs Puxley was succeeded by J A Houston, Yacht Builder, who in turn gave way in 1902 to Donyland Shipyard, Ltd.

In 1915 Harris Brothers, who built many famous yachts, some of them still afloat, ceased to operate and the Rowhedge Ironworks took a lease on their yard, which became the Lower Yard: it was purchased outright in 1943.

One thing revealed by the archives was that the master shipwright of the time tended to combine the operation with the ownership of one of the local beer-houses.

The three men from Swan Hunters on the Tyne never intended to compete with the illustrious yard that had trained them. They thought the opportunity existed to build smaller craft and over fifty years they have turned out 834 boats, many of them highly specialised. From the beginning the yard had to fight its way through trade depression: the first four years showed losses, so in 1908 the company was several times on the verge of winding up.

However, it was decided that if two of the directors sold out their interest, the third might be able to turn the corner, so Walter Oxton's father, a man of faith, bought the shareholdings of the other two and on 21 June, 1909, Oxton became the sole Managing Director.

In 1906 the total staff (workmen and apprentices) numbered 20, with a wage bill of £19 a week: by 1912 the wage bill was £140 weekly.

Walter Oxton had been born in Liverpool in

The 'Jackson Pasha', built by Rowhedge Ironworks, 1932, for the Sudan Government

1869 and was educated at Giggleswick School and the
Victoria University, Liverpool. He intended to be a
farmer, but served his apprenticeship as an engineer
and, before joining Swan Hunter, was employed as a
draughtsman by Thornewill & Wareham, Ltd., of
Burton-on-Trent. From 1904 until his death in 1937
he was at the helm of Rowhedge Ironworks.

The very first vessel from the yard was an out-
standing event, for no shipyard is successful until it
has something afloat. This achievement took the form
of a steel launch of 45 feet overall for James
Pollock, Sons & Company. She was named *Desterro* and
built for service in Brazil. She must have been
suitable, for later other boats were fashioned from
the same design. She was powered by a non-conden-
sing steam engine of the Ironworks own manufacture,
giving a speed of 9 m.p.h. She was an open boat with
a canopy overhead and a huge single funnel jutting
through, belching out smoke. Steered by a large ship's
wheel, she was doubtless useful on the tremendous
rivers of Brazil.

Another craft, built in 1908, was *The Prince of
Wales*, (Ship No.27), a pilot launch having another of
those special Rowhedge engines giving her a speed of
10.1 knots. This vessel was made for J A Smith for
service in the Thames Estuary and, although this was
many years ago, the general appearance, excluding
the then fashionable tall smokestack, would not dis-
credit a modern-day craft for the same duties.

Ship No.351 with sails (not of British design or
manufacture) was termed a gyassa and had no means
of auxiliary propulsion. Sixty feet long, this boat was
completed in 1926 for the Sudan Government for
service on the Nile. The outsize rudder bore a like-
ness to a Thames sailing barge, but the rig and
passenger accommodation would be considered too
primitive in this country. In contrast, owing little to
tradition, was Ship No.559, the steel Refuelling
Launch R.O.C.4. She was 50 feet 6 inches long, built

in 1937 for the British Tanker Co., Ltd., to carry
2,350 gallons of benzine and 200 gallons of lubricating
oil, for refuelling flying boats on a lake in Iran.
After trials, she was broken down into two sections
and shipped by steamer and overland for reassembly
on site. Diesel powered, she had a speed of 6½ knots.

At the beginning of World War II Rowhedge
built ships for the Crown Agents for the Colonies.
Ship No.529, of 84 feet, was driven by a twin
Gardner 8 L 3 diesel to give it a speed of 11¼ knots.
Intended for Customs in Nigeria, this very useful boat
was taken over by the Admiralty and did much in the
war as H M S *Umbriel*. After the conflict she was
handed back to the Crown Agents and is now working
in Nigeria, renamed the *Haussa,* her cruiser days just
a memory. Ship No.673 was called the *Hotspur IV* and
was a 69 ft ferryboat with cabins, a familiar sight on
the Southampton to Hythe run. Ship No.674, the *John
Hawkins,* was 64 feet long, with 295 h.p., and a
Thames tug, the third built for the same owner. She is
diesel powered.

After Walter Oxton died, Frank Butcher took
over as Managing Director: he had been apprenticed
in Colchester as an engineer and joined Rowhedge in
1907. When he died in 1946 Donald Oxton, son of
Walter, took over the firm, having passed through all
the departments of the Ironworks as an apprentice.

They built an interesting bulk tar carrier called
the *Target*. Tank heating coils kept the sticky tar
in fluid form during the sea passage. Ship No.467 was
the 80 ft *Dumb Spirit* tank barge, typical of the
many Rowhedge boats designed for overseas reassembly. Ship No.426 looked like a Mississippi paddle
boat with tiers of decks like a wedding cake; she
bore the name *The Nasir* and was a stern wheeler
made for the Sudan Government. She was 139 feet
long, but with a draft of only 3'6". A similar boat
called the *Rejaf,* another shallow draft stern wheeler,
was featured on a Sudan postage stamp, so pleased

The Walton Volunteer Lifeboat 'True to the Core II', built at Rowhedge. She was 40' long, carvel built and cost £473.

were they with her performance.

Ship No.99 was a paddle steamer of 70 feet called the *America,* being built for the firm's good customer Brazil: she was shipped out bodily. The *Omd - urman,* another shallow draft stern wheeler, built in 1929, had royal connections as it carried Edward, Prince of Wales, on one stage of his dash back to see his sick father, King George V, in 1935.

Another craft of which they were very proud was the *Wroxham Belle,* Ship No.528. She was fashioned for service on the Norfolk Broads, where she is still well remembered, for the Yarmouth & Gorleston Steamboat Co., Ltd., famous for its kippers. She could accommodate 180 passengers in a wide-windowed saloon, which had a retractable sunshine roof. Her function was that of a waterways coach. She was 80 feet long and had a speed of $7\frac{1}{2}$ knots. She was known for her easy manoeuvrability. She was requisitioned at the outbreak of war and saw service at Freetown: afterwards she was sold to Thames owners, for whom she is still operating.

Ship No.570 was a different kettle of fish. She was a wooden lifeboat of $35\frac{1}{2}$ feet named the *Guide of Dunkirk.* She was financed by funds raised by the Girl Guides and was originally intended to replace the St Ives lifeboat. She had many of the latest developments, including a double skin and a self-righting feature. Unfinished and still on the slips when news of the impending evacuation of Dunkirk was received in May, 1940, she was immediately launched and joined the fleet of little ships that snatched the British Expeditionary Force from the jaws of defeat.

They built sailing yachts too at the Lower Yard, one being the colourful *Tury* (Ship No.100), a steam yacht made in 1911 for James Pollock, Ltd., for a high South American dignitary. Resplendent with a highly polished brass funnel and a candy-striped awning, she reflected the status of her owner, even to the extent of having a small saluting cannon. $42\frac{1}{2}$

feet long and powered by an engine made at Rowhedge, she sped along at 8 knots. The *Umbrina,* over
76 feet long, was created in 1949 for Mr R Gilfillan,
an American living in Nairobi. She was one of the
largest private yachts built at the Yard since the War
and was a luxury yacht of the highest standard with
a Gardner 6L3 engine giving her 8½ knots. She was
launched flying the Stars and Stripes and ran her
engine within 10 minutes. After her sea trials she
was off on her 6,000 mile maiden voyage to her home
port of Mombasa.

Rowhedge did a lot for the modern yachting
enthusiast as well, Mr Robert Stone designing a half
decked centre-board sloop specially for the Yard,
called the *Firecrest Fifteen.* It was first introduced
at the 1950 International Boat Show and became a
regular production for the Lower Yard. It was named
after the celebrated round-the-world *Firecrest,* also
built at Rowhedge - in the 1920s - and circum-
navigated by the French lawn tennis star Alain
Gerbault.

Various vessels built in the yards were
classified as 'Top Secret'. The 50 ft steam pinnaces,
powered by engines from near neighbours of the time,
A G Mumford, Ltd., were supplied from 1912 to 1915
for service with such legendary boats as H M S *Tiger,
Delhi, Barham* and *Malaya.* The lethal little craft
were slung overboard from their parent ship and, by
what now seems very crude methods, went into the
attack with torpedoes. In the Great War a steel
steam tug of 80 feet was made by order of the War
Office for use on the Belgian canals. She was
powered by a Campbell & Calderwood C.S.C. engine
and could do 10 miles per hour.

The service craft built for the Admiralty during
World War II were numerous. Soon after the outbreak
they delivered three Mine Recovery Launches (Ships
602-4) to the order of the Turkish Government: made
of steel and galvanised, they were 60 feet long and

Miss Jones' snapshot of George V at Rowhedge Bridge

gave speeds of $9\frac{3}{4}$ knots, driven by 187 B.H.P. National Diesel.

Among the old-timers employed at the Yards were Ted Hudson, a timekeeper for many years, who lived up Darkhouse Lane in a cosy cottage. Another shipyard worker of many years was Reg Dixon, who lived in Chapel Street, while old Mr Spinks was once Shipwright Foreman down in the Lower Yard, where they fashioned the wooden vessels.

It was a sad day when the Ironworks closed for the last time in the early 60s. People walked about Rowhedge as if a funeral was in progress. Everything was lotted up and disposed of: Mr Hubbard bought the Upper Yard for his scrap metal business, while Mr I Brown got the Lower Yard, where he still carries on the skills of building and repairing lifeboats and yachts. The Village Council purchased some of the Quay, where there is now a nice green garden with seats overlooking the Colne.

Miss Jones, who lived in Ferry House in the High Street (from where her parents had run the ferry to Wivenhoe), related the history of the Great War Bridge.

It was built entirely of wood in 1914/5, with a section the opened in the middle to let larger boats use the tidal Colne. It was built to help transport military supplies along the east coast to Brightlingsea, Clacton, Frinton and Walton from the garrison depots in Colchester.

It was located opposite Mr Curle's old shop 'The London Stores', where Springetts, the grocers, is now. The Red Letter Day was when George V arrived on the Wivenhoe side of the river to inspect the bridge and he was 'snapped' by the daring Miss Jones with her box camera (you weren't supposed to take pictures of military objects in war-time!).

After the war the bridge was dismantled and, although the local Colnesiders had plenty of firewood for a time, the road journey to Wivenhoe is still via Colchester Hythe.

Fingringhoe

Fingringhoe is a delightful place full of old-world atmosphere. It is a pretty village with a duck pond, pure spring water and the ancient Whalebone public house. Its church of St Andrew is built chiefly of brick and stone and dates from the 15th century: it was much damaged in the Essex Earthquake of 1884 and during the subsequent repairs, several old wall paintings were disclosed, including the well-known subject of Michael weighing souls and another of the Mass of St Gregory.

The 15th century font has a good cover and an ironbound 'Dug Out' chest has the unusually late date of 1684: that is probably the date of its gift to the church, not of its construction.

There are many fine old Georgian houses here, one of the 17th century has good parquetry work and Jacobean wall painting.

But Fingringhoe is not just a pretty village: it has a strange history of smugglers, crooked vicars and an unusual mystery that made front-page news in the national papers of its time.

But to start at the beginning of Fingringhoe's written history...

The village is set on a low ridge running westwards from the tidal Colne and south of one of its tributaries, the Roman River. Its houses are scattered for more than a mile along a ridge road. The settlement dated from at least Roman times and excavations on Fingringhoe Wick on land owned now by the Essex Naturalists' Trust have uncovered the remains of three Roman villas. Under these were found relics of an earlier Claudian Roman invasion of Britain in A.D. 43. Archaeological finds at the Wick support the view that Fingringhoe was a Roman supply base and, perhaps, a fort for the garrison of Roman Colchester.

The name Fingringhoe is Saxon and in an Anglo-Saxon will of about 975 is written as Fingringaho. The name may mean Hoe for ridge of hill of Fingringas, the descendants or followers of a man the exact form of whose name is unknown, or, perhaps, from the old English word 'Finger', the reference being to the finger of land that diverts the Colne eastwards between the Roman River and Geedon Creek.

The church dating from Norman times was originally dedicated to St Ouen, a former Bishop of Rouen. The explanation is that in 1046 the Manor of Fingringhoe became part of the temporality of the priory of West Mersea, itself a cell of the French Abbey. This explains why the village is not mentioned separately in the Domesday Book, compiled under the orders of William the Conqueror in 1086.

Rev. Montagu Benton, vicar of Fingringhoe from 1922 to 1959, was a prominent local archaeologist, who considered that the substitution of St Andrew for St Ouen was due to an early 18th century misreading of St Awdeon or St Audoenus, alternative forms of Ouen. Mr Benton was also a member of the Central Council for the Care of Churches and was joint author of *The Church Plate of Essex* (Oxford University Press).

What a contrast with Fingringhoe's crooked vicar, Edmund Hickeringill, whom Benton calls the sole vicar of Fingringhoe to get a mention in the *Dictionary of National Biography*. He held the benefice in plurality from 1691 to 1703: as Benton discovered Hickeringill was notorious rather than distinguished.

In 1662 he became rector of All Saints, Colchester, where he remained - except for the years

1685-8 when he was excluded from his living - until his death in 1708.

Benton said he was 'eccentric and quarrelsome': a judgement proved by the slander case in which Hickeringill was involved in 1682, as a result of which he was ordered to pay the Bishop of London damages of £2,000, a fortune in those days. He was convicted of forgery in 1707. How he got away without being unfrocked is hard to imagine.

Until the Dissolution of the Monasteries the Manor of Fingringhoe was owned by the Master and Fellows of Higham Ferrers College. Thereafter the estate fell to the Crown and, in 1542, Henry VIII granted it, together with the rectory and advowson (right of presentation to the livery) to Robert Dacre and his heirs. For some unknown reason the estate reverted to the Crown, for in 1553 we read of Edward VI granting the Manor, rectory and advowson of Fingringhoe, besides that of Mersea and Peete Hall, to Thomas, Lord Darcy, of Chich (St Osyth).

The Dacre family remained the owners of the Manor for nearly a century and were responsible for the rebuilding of Fingringhoe Hall in the early 17th century.

In 1648 George Frere, a London merchant, purchased Fingringhoe and Peete Hall from Elizabeth, Countess Rivers, great-grand-daughter of Lord Thomas Darcy. She sold them for £1,000 of lawful 'monie of Englande.'

George Frere died in 1655 and has a monument in the church chancel, over the vestry door. The portrait seems to have been taken from a death mask. Below the inscription is a shield bearing the arms of the Levant Company, the famous English trading company formed in the late 1570s to control trade with Turkey and the eastern Mediterranean.

Frere left the Hall to his nephew John Goddard, who in 1707 sold it to Marmaduke Rawdon of Hoddesdon in Hertforshire.

A tablet on the north wall of the church nave erected to the memory of Mrs Hester Keeling traces the early 18th century history of the Rawdons and Keelings of the Manor.

Joseph Keeling, High Sheriff of Essex in 1765 and husband of Hester, held Fingringhoe Manor and lived in the Hall. He gave a fine coat of arms of the Stuart dynasty to the parish, which can be seen on the north wall facing the church entrance. This was restored by the College of Arms through the generosity of the last previous owner, Mrs J Furneaux. She was a wonderful character, often to be spied shooting through the neighbourhood in her small sports car with her two giant-size French poodles running behind. She donated Fingringhoe a football pitch.

Mr Val Stone, the Rowhedge artist, told an amusing story: it seems that years ago Mrs Furneaux and Col. Lindsay Smith (of Donyland Hall) each gave a book to the best two pupils of Donyland Church School and Fingringhoe School, as a joint effort to encourage learning.

The Hall was burnt down in the 1970s: today a doctor has restored the property and the massive hall looks very attractive.

The Spring is by the large duck pond, opposite the Whalebone. It must have been useful in the days before piped water as it was lovely and cool. Near the Spring was a giant oak tree: legend has it that a smuggler was buried there with an acorn in his mouth.

The picture-postcard Whalebone Inn is mostly 17th century with some Tudor origins. It is said there was a real whalebone arch outside the main door some years ago and also that it had connections, like all the marshland villages, with smuggling, being not far from the Colne. The venerable house is still open for trade.

Jabe Smith, a fascinating Rowhedge individual, tells a strange tale of Fingringhoe that turns out to

be the gospel truth. When he was a boy, he and his
local gang used to bike over to Fingringhoe, where
they found an old desolate, half-ruined cottage near
the Church and, like adventurous lads (little horrors!)
they decided to make it their headquarters in which
to hatch plans and generally play about. The deserted
cottage was quite small and some of the roof had
caved in, giving plenty of space for the elements to
enter, besides birds seeking to build their nests. Jabe
said there was a funny, damp smell, like rotting
leaves and timber and the abode had a spooky
atmosphere. They saw the remains of furniture and
other household items. For years they played there,
entering through a broken window, until one day
someone discovered some human bones on an old bed
covered with leaves. Jabe had his picture taken,
standing next to the local Bobby and it was front-
page news in the Essex papers. "Boys discover
skeleton" the headlines screamed and it created a lot
of public interest.

     The truth was that a retired music hall actress
named Connie Kent had lived there in retirement
after treading the boards for many years. She became
a recluse and was not a local person, so it seemed
nobody missed her, not even the milkman, if she had
one. It is thought she was probably taken ill and died
alone. They never could get to the bottom of this
particular tale and murder or foul play was suspected.
The inquest returned an open verdict. It was thought
that her remains had been lying there for some years.
Essex folk keep themselves to themselves with
strangers, so the cottage still held its terrible secret.
Today only the foundations remain to remind one of
the late Connie Kent.

     In front of the Kent cottage was the village
school which, in 1927, was just a small building
consisting of a hall and two classrooms, holding 32
boys and girls, not forgetting 40 infants. Since 1940
all children aged over 11 have been sent to other

schools in the area, like Rowhedge and Wivenhoe. But
the ferry which plied between the Wick and Wivenhoe
now is no more after centuries of operation, cut by
the modern economic trends.

One of the more prominent villagers in recent
years was Mr Geoffrey Abbot Green, who was known
as 'Buller' to his many friends. His nickname came
from General Sir Robert Buller, who played a major
role in the relief of Ladysmith in the Boer War.
During the celebrations following that operation, Mr
Green, then a young child, was exhibited from a
window in the top floor of Fingringhoe Hall and was
'christened' Buller by the villagers.

He had been born at the Hall and saw action
himself in the Great War, when he was commissioned
in the Infantry. When he returned to Fingringhoe he
farmed, first, at Holmwood and, later, at Picketts
Farm. He was a keen benefactor of the parish church
and gave the land where the vicarage was built. He
was an enthusiastic and courageous rider to hounds
and a keen walker, covering as much as 7 miles a
day when he was over 80. Mr Abbot Green came
from the well-known Essex farming family, of whom
many are listed in *Kelly's Directories* in the Victorian era. He died in 1983, aged 84, at a nursing home
in Rowhedge.

There are some charming old-world names in
Fingringhoe, like Pig's Foot Green, where once the
village blacksmith's forge stood - when Fingringhoe
was an innocent village.

The Fingringhoe Wick Reserve is a peninsular
of dense covered land, bounded by the Colne estuary
and the vast Geedon salt-marsh. It covers some 120
acres and was opened by the Essex Naturalists' Trust
in European Conservation Year, 1970.

It is open to the public at all times, being
especially popular at weekends, and a variety of wild
life can be observed. Birds like willow warblers,
blackcaps and whitethroats. During October it has

become a favourite place for migrants: flocks of sky-
larks, tree sparrows, starlings,, rooks, jackdaws and
wood pigeons, who fly over the estuary to the wick
where they turn westwards and either continue on
their journey or land to rest and feed.

Towards the end of July fresh hatches of
butterfly are seen, sunning themselves on the bramble
bushes with their wings fully open: Red Admirals and
Painted Ladies begin to appear on their favourite food
plants, the buddicia and the sedum.

In a mild March numerous adders and grass
snakes, as well as lizards, can already been seen.

Fingringhoe Nature Reserve is well worth a
visit; there is a clubhouse, with observation rooms, a
cafe, and a shop and bookstall.

The Whalebone, Fingringhoe: painting by E E Baxter

Abberton

Abberton is on the Layer Brook, near its confluence with the Roman River, only a few miles from Colchester on the road to Mersea Island. Its old English names were Aburton, Adburton and Adburgeton.

In Edward the Confessor's reign Siward, a freeman, and two other freemen enjoyed the lands of this parish. By the Domesday Survey the Lord of the Manor was Eustace, Earl of Boulogne, and his tenants were Ralph de Menci, Ralph Peverell and Odo under Suene: these were mostly Normans who had come over with the Conqueror and who had been rewarded for services rendered.

Earl Eustace was an ancestor of Queen Maud, consort of Stephen (1105-54), who had Rowhedge connections, as her father was the Duke of Boulogne.

By 1247 Olbert de Brightlingsey held the Manor from the King, while William de Montchenfi conveyed it to the Abbey of St Osthy (Osyth), which held it in pure alms for the heirs. In 1538 John Colchester, Abbot of St Osyth, conveyed the property to Sir Thomas Audley, the Chancellor of the Court of Augmentation. Audley did well out of the suppression of the religious houses in Essex and was granted a fine abbey at Saffron Walden, where his grandson built the splendid mansion of Audley End. Audley willed the main Abberton Manor to his brother for life and, after, to his nephew, also named Thomas Audley, and his heirs.

The Audleys are a fascinating Essex family,

rising from Lord Chancellor Audley who was born at
Earl's Colne in 1488 of obscure parents. He was
brought up in the law, made Town Clerk of
Colchester in 1516 and a free burgess in 1526. He
rose to become Autumn Reader of the Inner Temple
in London and was later Speaker of the House of
Commons in the Parliament that began on 3rd
November, 1529.

Henry VIII thought well of him and, in 1530,
Thomas Audley was made King's Attorney for the
Duchy of Lancaster. He advanced to ever higher posts
and never lost favour like the unfortunate Sir Thomas
More, whom he succeeded as Lord Keeper of the
Great Seal. In 1532 he was knighted and the following
year made Lord Chancellor.

Lord Audley was very zealous at the Dissolution
of the Monasteries and obtained from the King the
sites of St Botolphs Priory and the Crouched Friars in
Crouch Street, Colchester, together with other
valuable possessions in that town. In 1538 he reached
his peak and was created Baron Audley. He was
installed Knight of the Garter and died in 1544 at
the age of 60, being buried at St Mary's, Saffron
Walden, in a magnificent marble tomb.

Later in the history of the Manor Robert
Audley married Mrs Anne Packington, whose family
owned the other Abberton Manor of Badcocks, which
has a full history of its own. At the time of Domesday Badcocks was held by Ralph Peverell and Odo. In
1281 Alice Le Despenser, daughter and heiress of
Philip Baffet, had the Manor in the parish of
Adburgeton and Peltington (Peldon). With it she had
150 acres of arable land and four meadows, out of
which she paid 10 shillings a year to James de
Adburton, 14 shillings to William of Ranulph and
eighteen pence to the Ward of Stortford. Thomas
Springe was Lord of Badcocks Manor in 1523, with 26
acres called Bradfield and 12 called Tolmanis,
together with a tenement named Smythes - all leased

from the Dean and Chapter of St Paul's Cathedral, London.

The church register dates from 1703 and the church, though restored in 1834, is a 13th century foundation, with a western brick tower containing one bell.

In 1837 the population was 244 souls, living within 1,067 acres of loamy land, mostly arable.

White's Directory of 1863 shows that Thomas White was Lord of the Manor and resided at Abberton Hall. Miss Susan Sargent was the schoolmistress, William Smith the butcher and shopkeeper, and Tom Austin acted as miller and shopkeeper. John Benett was the local baker, while there were eight local farmers, including J Beardwell, Henry May and Tom Cooper, the latter working Badcocks.

By 1901 the vicar was the Rev C H Weaninck, whose benefice was £88 a year, the gift of the Lord Chancellor. At Malton House dwelt William Clary, cattle dealer, while Henry Harrison ran the local Post Office and was also a coach builder. Fred Ladbrooke did harnesses for the area and John Theobald was the boot and shoemaker. Although Abberton House was unoccupied in 1901, Mrs Hetherington was Lady of the Manor. The principal local landowner was Edmund Tom Hale, farming wheat, barley, oats and beans. The population had diminished to 199, including 50 children who attended the mixed school managed by Mrs E Thompson. Pantize Farm was worked by Francis Farr.

Now Abberton Manor has been transformed into a luxury nursing home with private grounds of 14 acres, but a hundred years before it had been lived in by E W Bawtree, Esq.

Abberton has never boasted a railway station, but even in 1909 Cox's *Guide for Essex* records that 'motor omnibuses run four times a day from Colchester Railway Station to Blackheath, Abberton, Peldon Corner and West Mersea.'

As regards local flora and fauna, the saltings house golden and marsh samphires, thrift, sea lavender, sea aster, sea blite and scurvy grass, while on other uncultivated areas sea campion, sea holly and wild celery can be found. On stretches of shingle and sand grow the horned poppy, sea rocket, sea kale and saltwort. The low marshland forms favourable feeding and breeding ground for numerous birds. Wildfowl are still numerous, though a mere fraction of those that formerly abounded. The Brent Goose can still be seen in severe weather. There are plenty of jays, starlings, and gulls, except the black-headed gull known locally as the Peewit gull. Both the raven and the woodpecker are seen less frequently than in the past.

As far as early human habitation is concerned paleolithic implements, now in Colchester Museum, have been found here in the shape of flint axe heads used by Stone Age man.

Abberton Reservoir covers a few square miles and, at its worst, can be like a rough sea, but the anglers make the most of it. Pike have been caught here weighing 38 lb and a dead fish of around 50 lb was found at the north-east of the reservoir bank. The water is also renowned for its shoals of bream and as a bird sanctuary, particularly wildfowl.

Colchester and the surrounding district draw their water from this large man-made lake.

Langenhoe

Langenhoe is a small scattered parish in the marshes
seven miles from Colchester between Abberton and
Peldon. The name comes from the Saxon, Langhou,
Lagenho and Lagenfo: the lang and hou means a long
hill.

In Edward the Confessor's day Ingecric had the
estate, while at the Domesday it was held by the
Earl of Boulogne, who had Langenhoe Hall, the manor
house near the church of St Mary. John le Despenser
and Mary, his wife, had two carveates of arable land
and 60 acres of woodland; perhaps this was rented
from the Earl.

The Lord Fitz-Walter was Lord of the Manor
until 1328: Lionel de Bradenhan held half a fee
(lease) and Lionel was a troublesome fellow. He
endeavoured to appropriate for himself the Geedon's
part of the Royalty of the River Colne, which
belonged to the Corporation of Colchester. Lionel
pretended it lay within his leased manor and enclosed
it with piles (poles). A commission was granted in
1362 and Robert de Harty, Lord Admiral, enquired
into the case. In 1364 Lionel, convicted of land-
stealing, was forced to seek pardon and a list was set
forth of his many felonies. It emerged that he had
beseiged Colchester for three months with 200 armed
men, attempting to burn it down! And, as if that was
not enough, he retained in his Langenhoe house
several thieves as his servants and had caused three
people to be drowned in the South Geedon Creek.

The Manor and the advowson of its church next

came into the hands of John de Sutton, son of Richard, his brother and others. The Suttons were from Wivenhoe. John held it on one knight's fee given to Walter, Lord Fitz-Walter, who died in 1396.

For the next 350 years nothing much happened, but by 1729 the Waldegraves held the Manor. They were an old Essex Catholic family coming from Borley and Navestock: there are monuments to various members of the family in Borley church. In 1887 the Lord of the Manor was still a Waldegrave - the Dowager Countess, wife of the Hon. Harcourt Vernon, but by 1900 the Lordship was held by Rt.Hon. Henry James Round, M.P., of Birch Hall, who also owned Pewett (now Peewit) Island [of 40 acres in the Pyfleet Channel between Mersea and the mainland]. The Rounds were also a well-known Essex family, who had once owned Colchester Castle: another contemporary Round was John Horace (1854-1928), one of the driving forces behind the *Victoria History of Essex.*

The church register dates from 1660, although there are earlier references. One was in 1597 when a Langenhoe man pleaded poverty to avoid becoming a churchwarden. The wardens' duties were heavy and manifold and the majority of parishes elected two wardens annually. Like modern jury service, you had to have a good reason for refusing the honour: old age was advanced on many occasions.

The old church of St Andrew was so entirely wrecked in the 1884 earthquake that a new church was built on the same site in 1886. The new church is of stone in the perpendicular style: it has an embattled west tower with pinnacles.

In 1887 the population of the parish was 234, with a rectory valued at £446, the acreage being 2,063. The vicar was Rev W Parkinson. In the parish there was a free school, endowed by Edward Mark in 1623, that had 2 acres of land; William Bennett was schoolmaster and parish clerk. In the village Robert

Hughes was the boot and shoemaker, while Mary Abraham was landlady of the 'Red Lion'. Farmers in the district included T S Cooper (The Hall), Thomas Green (Crouch House), Robert Kenett (West Farm) and Thomas Pertwee (Lodge Farm).

By 1900 the principle landowners were T D Pertwee and Joseph Procter. The size of the parish was then described as '2,071 acres of land, 13 of water, 239 of tidal water and 103 of foreshore': there was a population of 219. In the village the 'Red Lion' was now hosted by William James: Robert Brand was the coal dealer, J Hole the boot and shoemaker and James May was the village carpenter and undertaker.

The National School, built in 1878, had 50 boys and girls under the supervision of Miss Susan Parie.

A London man had a strange experience one night as he was duck-shooting in the freezing mud of the Pyfleet Channel, a lonely curlew-haunted waterway where years ago a now-lost and forgotten hard stretched through the fields of Langenhoe Hall. He saw the shadow of a man, seven feet or more tall, coming towards him in the mud: the apparition had a kind of winged helmet on and the shadow passed right over the terrified wild-fowler. Later, someone told him it was probably their old friend, 'Hasten the Dane', who habituates these parts - frightening strangers.

The Anglo-Saxon Chronicle tells us something of Hasten, a Danish King, of the ninth century. For we can read: "Soon after came Hasten to England with 80 ships into the mouth of the Thames and wrought him there a work at Milton and the other army at Appledore.

"The East-Angles had given oaths to King Alfred and the East Angles six hostages.

"Nevertheless, contrary to the truce as oft as the others, the plunderers went out with all their army. The Danes now seized much booty and would ferry it northward over the Thames into Essex to meet their ships.

"But the King's army rode before them and fought with them at Farnham, routed their forces and arrested the booty, and they flew over the Thames without any ford, then up by the Colne on an island.

"They wintered at Mersea because King Hasten was wounded and they could not carry him.

"Later Hasten was at Bamfleet with his gang, but was gone out to plunder when King Alfred's army arrived.

"The King's troops routed the remainder of Hasten's army and took all that was there, money, women and children, to London or Rochester.

"They also broke or burned some ships and took some to London, and Hasten's wife and two sons were brought before King Alfred who returned them to Hasten, because one of them was his godson, and the other Ealdorman Ethelred's. They had adopted them ere Hasten came to Bamfleet. When he had given them hostages and oaths and the King had also given him many presents, as he did also when he returned the children and wife."

At one time Langenhoe had a Red Hill, like Fingringhoe and East and West Mersea. These mounds, which abound on the borders of the creeks and rivers of the Essex coast, are not pre-Roman burial mounds. They rise to a height of from two to five feet and vary in size from $\frac{1}{2}$ an acre to $3\frac{1}{2}$ acres. They are certainly artificial, as their material is composed of burnt earth, which is sometimes mixed with coarse pottery and broken bricks.

Tidal embankments, camp sites, salt works, the burning of kelp for glass-making, have all been advanced as the causes for the formation of the 'Hills', but no-one knows for sure. The most plausible theory is that they were the sites of prehistoric potters' works. Many Red Hills have disappeared as the material was found useful in dressing clay lands, but at the turn of the century there were between 150 and 200 left in the county. They still await systematic archaeological exploration.

Cheese making was a regular and important industry of these marshland villages from time immemorial until about 1840. By far the greatest proportion of Essex cheese was made from ewes' milk; the marshlands and saltings of the coast and islands made admirable grazing for the flocks. At the time of the Domesday survey the Essex coast had over 18,000 sheep. The making of these sheep-milk cheeses was specially mentioned by the historians Norden and Camden in Elizabethan times. The first stated that 'They were sent all over England and abroad for the use of peasants and labourers'. The making of this cheese died out as a general practice about 1700, but after that date every good Essex house had its cheese loft for cow's milk cheese. The main reason Essex cheese is not sold today is the railways - for farmers found it more profitable to send fresh milk to the London markets rather than the processed material.

Agriculture stil flourishes in this part of Essex, judging by the number of farms in the corner south of the Colne. Fuller, in 1662, described Essex as a 'fair country plentifully affording all things necessary to man's subsistence'. So the rearing and fattening of cattle and sheep still continues, besides the growing of cereal crops.

Langenhoe Church

Langenhoe church has gone! There is only a wide vacant space in the churchyard where it had once proudly stood. Cox's *Guide for Essex* in 1909 stated "The church of St Andrew was so entirely wrecked by the Great Essex Earthquake of 1884, that a new one was built on the same site in 1886", while Nikolaus Pevsner's *Essex* in the Buildings of England series said in 1965 "St Mary, 1886, of old materials. Of the west tower, especially, much must have withstood the earthquake of 1884."

So what happened to Langenhoe church after that date?

In the 1886 rebuilding much of the old material was used, including the 500 year old doors, but the poor church lived an uncomfortable life thereafter - just as if it was living on borrowed time.

The Rev. Ernest Merryweather had been rector there for over 20 years before retiring to West Mersea. He later told local newspaper reporters that the church was haunted.

"I have had several psychic experiences there," he claimed shortly after his retirement. "One day I was walking through the church when the statue of St George coughed as I passed. I could scarcely bring myself to believe that a carved statue could cough. So I rushed out into the churchyard to see if there was anybody around, but the area was completely deserted."

On another occasion, Mr Merryweather was standing by the belfry tower wall when he heard a

voice saying, "You're a cruel man." He turned round
to see the penknife in his trouser pocket being
thrown on the floor - with the large blade open.
Later he found that a murder had been committed
there. The person reputed to have been murdered was
a woman, Lady Felicity, in the early days of the
original 15th century church.

Other strange things happened to Mr Merryweather, who seemed to collect ghosts like other
people do postage stamps. A woman was heard singing
in French in the building, while the church was
locked. The church bells often tolled by themselves,
when the church was shut, and he had seen an
apparition on more than one occasion.

Fired with enthusiasm the B B C sent a team
of ghost hunters to spend a night in the building in
1961, when the church had been closed for two years
with notices posted up warning 'of the dangerous
state of the building'. The team spent the night in
chilly silence, but the spirits stubbornly refused to
appear or otherwise co-operate. "You can't get
ghosts to order", commented Mr Merryweather at the
time.

Was this the most haunted church in Essex?
Perhaps Borley church and rectory hold this record,
but Langenhoe must surely come a close second.

After 1959 Langenhoe was never opened for
worship again. It stayed empty for three years, in an
ever-more dangerous condition. It soon looked like a
scene from *The Sleeping Beauty*, being overgrown
with weeds and creepers. It was a suitable place for
ghosts, with an air of desolate abandonment, but the
villagers of Langenhoe did not want their place of
worship pulled down. Local farmer Peter Wormell of
Langenhoe Hall carried on a particularly spirited fight
to keep the church, but the Chelmsford Diocesan
Authorities decided it should be demolished. Mr
Wormell took the matter to the Bishop himself, but
the death knell had already sounded for the church.

The Queen sealed the order for its demolition and the parish was united with Abberton. The graveyard was to be maintained by the Parish Council as part of the agreement. The medieval bell was transferred to Abberton church and the demolition gang came in 1962 to remove the local landmark that had parts going back 600 years.

It's sad that the church should survive for five hundred years until the earthquake of 1884 and then, after a mere 76 years, the new building should go.

St Mary's Church, West End, Langenhoe, c.1910

Peldon

Peldon, anciently known as Peltendon (meaning a hill) is on the Colchester-Mersea road. In 1086 it was in the lands owned by the Deacon of St Paul's Cathedral, London.

In 1282 Walter de Peltindone owned 360 acres and one windmill. Later Michael de la Pole, Earl of Suffolk and Lord Chancellor of England, held the Manor and one at Langham, but was forced to flee the realm and his estates were forfeited. In 1389 the banished Earl's son applied for a restitution of the estate and Manor of Peldon, but doesn't seem to have had his plea granted.

The Teye family got the estates in 1426 for four shillings a year, and in 1545 Henry VIII granted it to Sir William Petre and Ann, his wife. Sir Thomas Darcy, Viscount of Colchester, eventually got the Manor.

The church (St Mary the Virgin) was much restored in 1859, but was originally mainly 15th century, with chancel, nave and embattled west tower. During restoration various traces of early Norman work with Roman tiles was uncovered.

In *Elizabethan Life, Morals and the Church Courts,* by Dr F G Emmison, Peldon gets quite a few mentions.

With the reissue on 1559 of Edward VI's Act of Uniformity by which the use of the Prayer Book became obligatory again, Elizabeth's first Parliament decreed compulsory church attendance for everybody above 14 on all Sundays and holy-days. A fine of 12 pence was to be levied by the churchwardens on every person defaulting, and this was to be used for the poor.

The Act of Uniformity also enjoined all members of the congregation 'then and there to abide' for the entire service and sermon. Late arrival or early departure was an offence and some delinquents created minor disturbances by so doing. The prize surely goes to John Laurence of Peldon in 1597 'for going out of church before the sermon ended to charm a thorn out of a maid's leg'. This he denied, saying that he 'was sent for by Goodwife Westbrowne of Abberton to do the matter he is accused of'. So he was given the chance of purging with four friends.

People were fined by the church courts for permitting swine and other animals to stray into the churchyard. The same John Laurence of Peldon was presented in Court in 1600 because 'his sheep were in the Peldon churchyard and did defile it, so that it was noisome to the whole parish when they went to church'. John Laurence explained, "The churchyard did lie open so as a few sheep to the number of three or thereabouts were there, but there were a hundreth of other folks."

The statutory duty of church attendance included receiving the sacrament on days when Holy Communion was administered - usually Easter, Whitsun and Christmas. Absence from Communion, however, was a separate offence. Every parishioner was required to partake of the Lord's Supper at least three times a year. In 1593, at the Church Court session, 40 Peldon villagers were cited for not receiving Communion, but the circumstances were exceptional insofar as the reason was 'through the sickness of their minister'. A somewhat illogical prosecution; puzzling too, as the rector, William Teye, was himself also accused at the same time for not wearing the surplice and not saying the litany, the epistles and the gospels. The next month nearly all the Peldon defendants attended and had to pay the Court fees. After that they do not seem to appear again, so it may be assumed that there was little or no further cause for complaint.

In 1597 William Evans of Peldon was before the Archdeacon's Church Court for 'brawling and quarrelling with the minister of Easter Day in the church and churchyard; he did draw his dagger on the minister.'

The most strange case concerned licences. By Royal Injunction of 1559 nobody was allowed to teach children openly in a school or private house without a licence from the ordinary. Schoolmasters had to take an oath of Royal Supremacy. On some occasions the Archdeacon's Courts considered charges involving pedagogues who acted as if ordained ministers. John Knight, rector of Goldhanger, was censured in 1588 for 'suffering the schoolmaster, who is a mere lay-man, to preach at church'. On appearing the vicar explained that 'thinking Mr Parker to be a minister and a preacher, being as hath sithence learned that he is not, did suffer him to preach' and he added that Parker was 'commended to him by Mr Drabye, the Bishop of Norwich'. Parker was, in fact, a school master of Peldon. A few months later he told the judge that 'whatsoever they do, he will not leave his calling without the Word of God'. At the same session William Teye, Rector of Peldon, was accused of 'receiving Mr Parker to the Communion, knowing that he was then excommunicate'.

The Rose Inn, of Tudor origin, figures in Sabine Baring-Gould's classic Essex novel *Mehalah;* there the unfortunate girl, fallen on hard times, sought work. The Rose is one of the most attractive inns in Essex and is still open for trade.

Smugglers had a false bottom to the duck pond adjoining the Rose, where they stored all manner of contraband goods - tubs of rum, Holland gin, and

The Rose Inn, Peldon

even rolls of silk. Also in that duck pond, where Carolinas and Mandarins quack today, the kegs were sunk with stones, then covered with a layer of soil to hoodwink the Revenue men into believing the bottom was level. Sometimes blocks of salt were used to sink the barrels: some days later the salt would have dissolved and the kegs floated to the surface to be collected by the watchful smuggler.

Essex abounds with ghost stories and Peldon has its fair share. Old Mrs Jane Pullen was landlady of the Rose before the last war. The pub stands at the crossroads where the Roman Causeway, known as The Strood, runs straight in true Imperial fashion across the saltings and sea-channels to Mersea island. Mrs Pullen walked home one night from Mersea, across the moonlit Strood, when a most strange thing happened. She heard footsteps behind and they were not the clumping steps of men in farm boots or the soft thudding of a fisherman with his rubber water-boots, but the ringing, clanging steps of a man in armour, swinging along at a ruthless march. Just like the Romans marching proudly behind their brazen eagles from Meresaia, their island. Mrs Pullen rushed home never daring to look behind.

Today they will tell you of the long shadow that walks in the moonlight. Some say it is a Roman centurion; others claim that on one night in each year there is fought, on the sea-wall, a clashing duel between a Viking from the northern seas and a Roman soldier – fighting to the death!

In 1863 Peldon was described as a low salt-marsh place near Mersea Island, over which the church tower commanded a view of the ocean. The population was 501. Large landowners were J Pledger, J Bawtree and A Taylor. The Rectory was a small manor lived in by the Rev. C R Harrison. A small fair was held in the village on Michaelmas Day. There was a National School, of which Miss H Wright was mistress. The church had five acres of land in 1863,

Crossing the Strood, 1920s

but the parish had no deeds relating to it! The village
blacksmith was John Cook, while William Cook kept
the Post Office. Henry Cooper was the baker, and
Thomas Gladwell the thatcher. The Lord of Peldon
Manor was Henry Thomas Tiddleman.

By 1874 the school had 110 pupils and was
enlarged in 1881: the schoolmaster then was A Green.
The parish clerk was Thomas Talbot. Carriers to
Colchester were W Christmas and G Nicholas, running
from Peldon to the Plough Inn, Colchester, on
Mondays, Wednesdays, Fridays and Saturdays.

Peldon Church

The Earthquake

The Great Essex Earthquake will not be easily forgotten in the north and east of the county. It occurred at eighteen minutes past nine on the morning of Tuesday, 23rd April, 1884, and was severely felt in the district between Colchester and the Blackwater. It was the most serious earth tremor that had happened in the British Isles for about four centuries.

The number of buildings damaged by the shock was 1,244, including 20 churches and 11 chapels, the main area of damage being from Wivenhoe to Peldon. St Mary's church, Peldon, was much damaged, as was the Rose Inn, where a portion of the roof was destroyed, bad cracks appeared in the walls and a large chimney toppled to the ground.

The extent of the chaos at Abberton was very noticeable, the village constable stating that hardly a house escaped damage. Observers estimated that not more than half a dozen chimney stacks remained intact, while on the Peldon to Abberton road not one undamaged chimney was visible.

Abberton House, owned by J Bawtree, underwent considerable shock and the chimney stacks, retaining their equilibrium, turned partly round. Many tiles were removed from Abberton church.

At the Abberton Lion (or the Langenhoe Lion, as it is on the parish boundaries), a chest of drawers hurtled across the room.

The offices of the *Essex Telegraph* in Colchester, also slightly damaged, were beseiged by towns-

people eager for information. Some assumed that a
town gas-mains had exploded.

At Langenhoe, besides damage to the church,
some outbuildings at Wick Farm were completely
destroyed, while the roofs were almost removed from
Langenhoe Hall and Crouch Farm. Other buildings
damaged in this locality were Pett Tye, Rolls and
Pantiles Farm.

The Bell Inn of Old Heath village, now a
suburb of Colchester, was wrecked completely. In
Rowhedge slates fell off the church roof and in the
old rectory cottages a falling chimney killed little
Mary Richer - the only human victim of the
catastrophe. In the High Street brewery a huge tank
shifted and turned over - all the male workers had
free beer.

The local newspapers reported that Peldon
church had reopened for services on 4th January,
1885. The local vicar, Rev. C Hall, was unable to
take the service because of illness, so his place was
taken by Rev. Robert Hunt, Secretary to the British
and Foreign Bible Society in Oxford. The east and
west walls of the church had been split in the earthquake and the arch partly gave way. There were also
many cracks in the nave and chancel walls and the
restoration work, carried out by Mr Letch of Brain-
tree, cost £470. This, the *Essex County Standard* reported, would come from the Mansion House, London,
Relief Fund, which had subscribed £8,906.14s, which
was chiefly distributed amongst the 381 private
owners who needed the most assistance in the repair
of their property.

In *Kelly's Directory* for 1902 the Vicar was
listed as Rev. David Lindsay, M.A., who dwelt in the
rectory. Mr Thompson had Butler Farm, while Brick-
house Farm was in the hands of William Fairhead.
Gaius Fosket was a Peldon Hall Farm, as well as
being a big landowner. The village grocer was
S Hyham and the Plough Inn and the Rose Inn were

managed by Fred Hill and George Pullen respectively. I believe the lady scared by the ghost in armour on the Strood nearby was the latter's wife who, after his death, carried on as landlady of the Rose.

G Simpson was the local builder and the Post Office and bakers was in the hands of G Smallwood. Fred Smith was the miller, although the mill was over the Strood in West Mersea: it had been established in Victorian times and was in the family for many generations. Smith was described as both steam and wind miller.

These Essex communities have developed much in the past eighty years! There is now a daily bus service run by Eastern National and Colchester Corporation and nearly every house has electricity, gas and mains water. Telephones and cars are plentiful. Small estates of semi-detached houses have recently been erected, but these are still pleasant farming areas. The lonely marshlands bordering the villages are full of wild birds, flowers and beauty, with the sweet tang of an Essex sea-filled air.

Mersea Island

Mersea Island is only nine miles from Colchester and is today often called a town, but to locals it will always be known as the villages of East and West Mersea. The island is connected to the mainland by the pre-Roman causeway of The Strood, submerged at high tides. The ghosts of Roman soldiers have been seen on The Strood, possibly because the island was a noted convalescent place during the long Roman occupation.

The island is five miles long and two miles wide. In 1909 the population was 1,524; now it has passed 10,000. The island is shaped like an oyster and the Musset family are famous here for rearing oysters, many a delicious native being eaten at Colchester's Annual Oyster Feast. They can be bought by the public for Musset's stall is down on the hard, close to the glittering sea dotted with sailing boats and pleasure craft.

There are 5,322 acres of arable and pasture land, besides the saltings.

The land round here is known as 'Mehalah Country', *Mehalah* being the stirring novel of the island by Sabine Baring-Gould, who was vicar at East Mersea for a number of years. Men can still be seen prowling around with guns, but nowadays wildfowl is the only quarry sought and it is not necessary to emulate Mehalah and carry a gun in self-defence.

And, though you may find neither the 'small farmhouse built of tarred wreckage timber and roofed with red pan-tiles' on that little Mersea island called

The Cottage near the Mill, West Mersea

The boy is Preston Smith, whose family worked Smith's Mill, 1898

Ray Island (which formed the heroine's home in the story), nor the dismasted vessel fastened upright by chains, the keel sunk in the shingle ('on the Mersea beach in which George de Witt lived with his Mother'), you may find several buildings and boats which might well have been the originals of those described by Baring-Gould. In any case the search will have fully demonstrated the wonderful scenic descriptions in the book: the pen pictures of the marshes and saltings of Mersea show what a deep impression those features had made on him. Baring-Gould's other claim to fame is as the writer of 'Onward Christian Soliders'.

West Mersea church is dedicated to Saint Peter and Saint Paul, like so many others in this corner of Essex. The walls are of ragstone, Roman bricks, septaria and sundry other materials. The West Tower is a good example of Saxon work and is entered from the nave by a very splendid Norman archway. On the east and west walls are remains of medieval paintings. The font is unusual in having a Norman bowl, supported by a fragment of a Roman pillar.

There are two notable chests in the square tower; one is 16th century with big lock-plates and staples, the other has fine ornamental hasp-plates and, being leather-covered, is probably 17th century. The Church Register dates from 1738.

Roman remains are common in this part of Essex and West Mersea was the site of an important settlement. Early in the 18th century a splendid tessellated pavement was discovered immediately to the west of the church, where the roadway now runs. A further discovery was made 200 yards to the east of the church: it was the foundations of a circular building of Roman construction. Doubts exist as to the form and purpose of the superstructure, which might have been a lighthouse, a monument or a tomb. The foundation is of rather unusual design.

The eastern part of Mersea, in Edward the

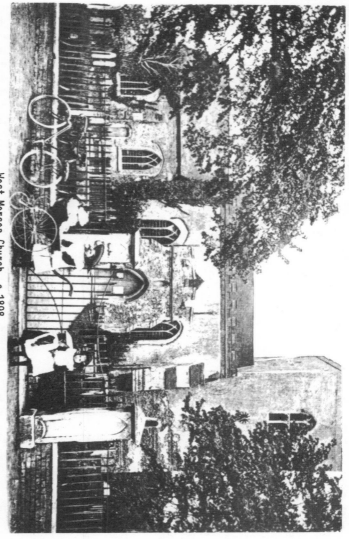

West Mersea Church, c.1898

Confessor's time, belonged to Robert, son of Wimarce, and, later, to Suene, his son, at the time of Domesday.

In 1210 and 1211 Richard de Rivers held the estate and Manorship of East Mersea, in honour of Hagenet: it was let to him by King John and was worth £15 a year. William de Rivers held it when he died in 1276, while John, his son, died only two years later, leaving the lordship to his son, William, who was under age and in wardship to Giles de Fenes. In 1325 Sir Richard de Rivers had the manorship and was styled 'Lord of East Mersey'.

The estate passed through a number of hands after this, including the Swinbornes, the Findernes, the Wentworths, the Bellamies and the Creffields. Sir Ralph Creffield, knight of Colchester, purchased the estate in 1748. He had no male issue, so Thamar, his only daughter and heiress, conveyed it by marriage to James Round, son of William Round of Birch Hall.

The Romans were the first to recognise the importance of guarding the Colne Estuary at East Mersea, as they had a whole fleet of boats there to repel invaders. A thousand years later about 1540 East Mersea had a fort or blockhouse on the south-eastern tip of the island called the Stone: it is first mentioned in 1547.

Its importance was again recognised at the time of the Civil War. Parliament, on receiving a request from the Borough of Colchester that the town should be better fortified, presented it with £1,500 for the town's defences and also a garrison at East Mersea. At the start of the siege in 1648 (the town was held by George Goring, Earl of Norwich, for the King) the Parliamentarian leader, General Fairfax, wanted to ensure that the Royalists received no outside help. First Fairfax encircled the town (which was parliamentary in its sympathies even though commanded by Royalists) and then sent a troop of dragoons to capture East Mersea fort. One hour after its seizure a strong detachment of Royalists arrived on Mersea, but they were too late and left without a fight. A few days later two Royalist frigates, of ten and eleven guns respectively, tried to enter the Colne mouth carrying provisions and arms to relieve the Colchester garrison, but the Parliamentarians sent attacking ships from Harwich and a battle followed. The Parliamentary ships were helped by the troops from the Mersea blockhouse and the Royalist ships were soon boarded and taken. The gunfire was heard in Colchester and Lord Goring sent a troop of horse downriver through the enemy lines, but again they were too late.

This was the deciding factor in the Essex part of the Civil War, for now no supplies could reach Colchester. Bravely the town held out for 76 days, the townspeople being reduced to eating horses, dogs and cats, as well as rats. When they surrendered Fairfax ordered them to pay a fine of £14,000 - or have the town plundered by his troops.

After this the importance of the Mersea fort diminished and, in 1651, repairs to the fort were ordered, but never carried out. By 1710 it had almost disappeared and only a few pieces of cannon and debris remained. The remains were finally cleared away when the sea-wall was built in the 19th century. Today the only reminders of the fort are two grassy embankments on the seaward direction about 150 feet long.

East Mersea church is set amidst corn fields that run down to the sea and is dedicated to St Edmund. It is of less account historically than West Mersea church, but its most interesting feature is its situation within a moated area, where 'the Danes took refuge after their defeat by Alfred at Farnham'. The embattled western tower was garrisoned by troops during the Dutch and French wars of the seventeenth century. The massive iron door at the foot of the staircase should be noted, as should the

Queen's Corner, West Mersea, c.1912

rood loft stair and the old pulpit with its sounding
board, which commands the pews though it is no
longer used. In Tudor times it was reported to the
Archdeacon's Church Court that at both East and
West Mersea 'the churchyard pale is rooted up by
hogs shamefully'.

East Mersea will always be associated with
Sabine Baring-Gould. In 1871 his vicarage at Dalton
was growing too small for his ever-increasing family,
which eventually reached 15 childen, so Mr Gladstone
offered him the living of East Mersea, where Baring-
Gould was incumbent for 10 years. *Mehalah* was pub-
lished in 1880. Later, in a book entitled *Further Rem-
iniscences*, Baring-Gould wrote rather uncompliment-
arily of his life at Mersea, saying, "My impressions
were that generations afflicted with those complaints
[ague and rheumatism] had lowered the physical and
mental development of the islanders.' He did not
suffer fools gladly and wrote 'As far as I could see
there were not many persons of value as readers and
thinkers, with whom to make friends'. Baring-Gould
thought Mr Musselwhite, the vicar of West Mersea, to
be a kind man, but not possessed of many interests
or of much information.

He liked Cant, an intelligent farmer and a
strong Dissenter, but stated that most of the other
local farmers only concerned themselves with eating
and drinking. As for the children of the parish, most
were uncouth and some of the parents were very
poor. It was not unusual to see the children decked
out in second-hand discarded military uniform, cut
down to the required size.

Older original inhabitants of Mersea will tell
you that Mehalah, the fictional heroine of Baring-
Gould's novel, was based on a real Mersea girl, the
daughter of Billy Baker, the ferryman, by his first
wife. The girl eloped with a soldier called Gardner or
Gardiner from Colchester garrison. In his auto-
biography Baring-Gould wrote of the girl's parents.

He was in the habit of taking the East Mersea ferry
over the Colne estuary to visit Brightlingsea and
therefore knew Baker. Billy Baker dwelt on East
Mersea hard with his wife in an old hulk of a ship
drawn up on the shingle and permanently anchored
there. Sometimes Billy's wife rowed passengers across
and Baring-Gould often took tea with them in their
strange home. Billy's wife was often tipsy, although
Baker was himself a sober man. Mrs Baker wore an
old military coat over her back, shoulders and arms.

East Mersea rectory was an old windswept
place with ill-fitting windows and doors. It was
shaken up in the Eathquake of 1884 and pulled down
in the early 1900s.

Baring-Gould left for the west country in 1881
and his successor was A L Hunt, 'Low Church' and
better liked by the islanders.

The main curiosity of Mersea is, without doubt,
the Barrow, of which many strange tales have been
told. Not far from The Strood, this ancient tumulus
stands over 20 feet high and, boasting a diameter of
more than 100 feet, resembles a small hill. Mehalah
was told the following tale about the Barrow by
Elijah Rebow -

'"In olden times when the Danes came here
they wintered on Mersea Isle and in summer they
cruised all along the west coast, burning and
plundering and murdering.

"There were two chiefs, both brothers, who
were very close. They were twins born in the same
hour and they had but one heart and soul. What one
willed so willed the other, what one desired so
desired the other also.

"One spring they sailed up the nearby creek, at
St Osyth's on the other side of the Colne Mouth, and
there they took the beautiful St Osyth and killed her.
She had a sister very pretty too, and she fell to the
lot of the brothers.

"They brought her back to Mersea and then

each would have her for his own. So the brothers fell out over the maiden and all their love turned to jealousy and hatred.

"And it came about that they fought with their long swords, who should have the maid. They fought and smote and hacked one another until their armour was broken and their flesh was cut off and their blood flowed away and by nightfall they were both dead.

"Thereupon the Danes drew their ships up to the top of the hill, just above The Strood, and they placed the lovely maiden in the hold with a dead brother on either side of her in his tattered harness, sword in hand, and they heaped a mountain over them and buried them all; the living and the dead together. (Which was very unfortunate for the poor native girl)."

Rebow paused and pointed to the moon hung over the hoe.

"When the new moon appears," he said, "the flesh grows on their bones and the blood staunches and the wounds close and breath comes back behind their ribs.

"When the moon is full, they rise in the ship's hold and fall on one another, and, if you listen at full moon on the hoe, you can hear the brothers fighting below in the heart of the barrow. You hear them curse and cry out and you hear the clash of their swords.

"But when the moon wanes, the sounds grow fainter, their armour falls to bits, their flesh drops away and their blood oozes out of all the hacked veins and all is still.

"Then when there is no moon you can hear the maid mourning and sobbing; you can hear her quite distinctly, till the new moon reappears and then she is hushed, for the brothers are recovering for a new fight..." '

In 1912 the Barrow was excavated by the

Morant Club of Essex. No trace was found of maiden, brothers or ship, but they found in the centre of the barrow a small chamber about 18 inches square by 22 inches high. In it was a lead casket, about a foot square and deep and covered with two pieces of board, containing a glass bowl, 11½ inches high and nearly 13 inches across, which in its turn held the cremated remains of an adult, probably a Romano-Briton of good position, dating from the first half of the first century A.D.

The story of the Danes staying on Mersea is certainly true. As the *Anglo-Saxon Chronicle* records:

"In A.D.895 the Danes out from North Wales, with the booty they acquired there, they marched over Northumberland and East Anglia, so that King Alfred's army could not reach them, they came into Essex eastwards, on an island that is out at sea, called Mersey.

"Then the same year, before Winter, the Danes who abode in Mersey, towed their ships up the Thames and Lea."

Mersea was granted to the Abbey of St Ouen by Edward the Confessor in 1046 and a small priory was founded there. It was suppressed as an alien house by Henry V and its possessions were granted by Archbishop Henry Chicheley to the college he was founding at Higham Ferrers, Northamptonshire.

West Mersea had five manors at one time: on the Dissolution of the Monasteries they came to the Crown and the chief manor of West Mersea was granted in 1542 to Robert Dacres, who died the next year, leaving the estate to his son, George, who was under age. In 1553 the manor was granted by Edward VI to Thomas, Lord Darcy, of St Osyth, and it was held by the family for many years.

Thomas, who owned other estates at Fingring-hoe, Rowhedge and Colchester, asked Edward VI to grant him the properties of St Osyth and Clacton, which had been given to Princess Mary. Accordingly,

we find the future Queen of England writing to her
half-brother on 6 December, 1552 –

"And wheare your Majestyes pleasure to desyre
is to have of me in exchange for another land the
Manor of St Osythes, Little and Great Clacton and
Wylleighe and their appurtenances, I shall most
humbly with all my whole harte and wyll obeye and
satisfye your hyghnes pleasure and desire in that
behalf.

"Your Majestye's moste humble sister Mary."

The following May Lord Thomas Darcy
received, by Royal Grant, 'the Manor of Clacketon,
the Parks of Alton and Clacketon, the Rectories of
Clacketon Magna, Clacketon Parva and Little Holland-
on-Sea'. The Darcy arms are still on the heraldic
badge of Clacton-on-Sea. The Darcy family descended
from a D'Arcy who came to England with William
the Conqueror, the family settling in Essex. Tolleshunt
D'Arcy is named from them.

Thomas lived at the former priory of St Osyth
and this, and the Manorship of West Mersea, passed
to his son, John. His daughter Elizabeth was made
Countess of Rivers, marrying Sir Thomas Savage, but
being widowed young. She was a patron of the arts,
helping John Wilbye (1572-1638), who has sometimes
been described as the 'Father of English Music'. The
Countess fell upon difficult times in the Civil War and
was obliged to sell her West Mersea estate in 1649 to
John Kidby, M.A., Rector of Shenfield.

The Church Courts of Elizabethan times
mention Mersea on many occasions. In 1597 there is
an incidental reference to a 'parish notice'. Nicholas
Wright of West Mersea, brought to Court, said: "Being
Constable and Surveyor, he gave warning to the parish
to come to amend the highways upon a certain day
whereof Richard Foakes and James Donnying now
deceased did laugh him to scorn. Whereupon he did
ask them what they meant thereby and he wished the
churchwardens to present the same; instead of which

The Victory, West Mersea, c.1900

the wardens presented Wright, their version being that he 'brawled in church after evening prayer'."

A rewarding walk is along the Coast Road, by the sea, known locally as the Blackwater. On Mersea hard, near the modernised Victory Inn, are many old famous sailing yachts, now used as houseboats, including one once owned by King Alfonso of Spain: once crewed by Rowhedge men, she now looks a wraith of her glorious past, never again to race, carrying the crowned heads of Europe aboard her.

Further along the Coast road are some curious brick and weatherboarded Essex fishermen's cottages, set back from the road in a kind of square over-looking the sea. Mrs Nelly Wilsmore was born in one of them and can recount memories of the 1900s. She was formerly of the Musset family (previously mentioned) and when she was a 'gal' in about 1910, she used to hawk a bend of fish around West Mersea village. A bend was a stiff piece of wire strung with fish, like a fishy necklace, and usually cost sixpence [2½p]. So Nelly would cry "Buy my fresh fish", just like the London hawkers.

Down the Hard or Coast Road 'The Lane' surprises the visitor: it is so quaint with houses of all periods. A wooden weatherboarded and tiled building, called 'Nutshell Cottage', catches the eye: this must be one of the smallest residences in Essex, if not England. As you stroll by, you can glance in the up-stairs front bedroom window, it is so low. A collection of huts near here was once referred to as 'The City' by the locals, who must have had a sense of humour! Smith's windmill has long since vanished from the West Mersea townscape.

In recent years Mersea has boasted many local personalities.

Captain Hudson lived in a house overlooking the Hard and Blackwater. He took Shackleton to the Antarctic in 1913 to search for Robert Falcon Scott and, later, did a lot for the Mersea community. His daughter, Ann, has a special place in her heart for Mersea and is often in residence in her caravan.

Another well-known resident was Albert James Carter of West Mersea Boatyard. Mr Carter was known as Bert to his friends and spent nearly all his 82 years on the island. On leaving school he became an apprentice shipwright to the Southampton company of Camper & Nicholson, and then returned to Mersea. He went to sea for a period, but in the 1920s joined Jim Clarke in buying the boatyard on Coast Road from A J Hampstead.

In World War II Clarke & Carter had a number of Admiralty contracts to supply oars and landing nets, thus keeping quite a big local labour force. At this time Mr Carter was a member of Peldon Home Guard. After the War the boatyard enlarged and the company started building yacht spars and masts, until they were superseded by the new lightweight version. In the 50s the saltmarshes, opposite the Victory Inn, were filled in to give hard standing. Clarke & Carter was sold to Nicholas and Barry Griffin in 1972, but even in retirement Mr Carter was active. He owned an oyster lane and trawled and dredged in his CK 99 fishing boat called *The Ann*. He was on the Mersea Regatta Committee, vice-president of the local football and cricket clubs, a freemason and founder of West Mersea Bowls Club.

A writer living at West Mersea is Hervey Benham, who has written many East Coast books on sailing, fishermen, bargemen and maritime history, with such titles as *The Last Stronghold of Sail* and *The Codbangers* - the story of the Icelandic and North Sea cod fishermen in the days of sail.

While on a literary note at Mersea, I feel that the modern thriller Writer, Margery Allingham, deserves a mention. Besides writing thrillers (*Mystery Mile* having a very Mersea-like setting), she wrote a novel based on the Island entitled *Blackkerchief Dick*, a strong character who indulged in a bit of smuggling on the quiet. Margery Allingham lived in nearby Tolleshunt D'Arcy from the mid 30s till her death, in a graceful Georgian house, formerly the home of Dr John H Salter.

Dr Salter was a proper Essex worthy and often made rambles to the Mersea district. He was a diarist, a prominent Freemason, a sportsman and a sportsdog breeder (who owned in his lifetime 2,296 dogs of 44 breeds, winning 611 prizes at shows).

An Essex guide of 1930 said: "Among islands in the county, Mersea is exceeded only in size by Canvey near Southend. It's surprising how many strangers express amazement on finding Mersea well provided with luxuriant trees and, in parts, quite hilly. There are three inns, a hotel, and a number of houses displaying the magic word 'Apartments'.

"The principal industries of the inhabitants are in connection with the oyster fisheries and agriculture and in ministering to the wants and requirements of the sailing men, with whom the place is so popular. At one time the neighbouring waters were also famed for soles.

"Yes, Mersea is a well-known welcome haven to sailing men; it has abundant anchorages, though its freedom is somewhat restricted by the oyster beds. Anchoring in Calcutt Channel or between Cobmarsh and Packing Marsh Islands is prohibited.

"With the increase of motoring, Mersea has become very popular with the landsman, his wife and family and those with a leaning towards out-of-the-way spots; it can be highly recommended. There is unlimited bathing, boating and fishing; there are tennis courts and within easy reach are the cinemas and bright lights and other allurements of Colchester and Clacton-on-Sea."

That was Mersea in the 30s and it hasn't changed much, except to grow, like 'Topsy'. Now there are a good variety of shops and superstores, a public library and banks, a handy post office and

yachting stores. Some select, well-placed caravan
sites blend in with the local scenery, while modern
housing estates have been well carried out.

I like the local Mersea Museum, opened in the
last decade near West Mersea church - and now they
boast a Health Centre - but still no main line gas!

'The City', West Mersea

Salcott-cum-Virley

Not far from Mersea Island, up the Salcott Channel, are the twin villages of Salcott and Virley: if ever there was a smugglers' haunt, this surely is it. Slip up the Salcott Channel (now rather silted up and little more than a stream) under cover of night and unload the contraband near the bridge (once wooden) that links the two parishes, like The Bridge of Sighs.

If you stand at the crossroads at the end of Salcott Street (where the B1026 main road to Maldon is rejoined), you can look up Barn Hall Road towards the scene of some very ghostly happenings, many years ago, in the Tolleshunt Knights area.

In ancient times there were supposedly some Satanic Rites and Practices held here, presided over by the 'Devil' himself. These strange rites were held on the banks of a bottomless pond in the nearby wood, still known as Devil's Wood.

Another curious tale connected with the crossroads is that of 'Black Shuck'. He was a demon dog and often makes his appearance there and he is, in some parts of East Anglia, held to be the Devil himself in a canine form. Black Shuck gets his name from 'Scucca', the Anglo-Saxon for demon. He walks alone and terrorises unsuspecting people travelling through lonely places, howling and shrieking fiendishly. The Essex Shuck is reputed to be different to the Suffolk, Norfolk and Cambridge versions. Unlike the others, he is a kindly hound and only haunts the sites of ancient gallows and graveyards. Otherwise he protects travellers on lonely, isolated roads. His

similarity to the others is his form: that of a massive
hound who salivates fire from his mouth. Once seen,
he will vanish from view as swiftly as he first
appeared.

Essex is full of groups of villages with a
common name. Hereabouts are three Layers, three
Tolleshunts, four Colnes and three Teys, also Little
Wigborough and Salcott Wigborough. The village we
know as Salcott was formerly a hamlet of Great
Wigborough and, as it was so far from the mother
church of St Stephen in Great Wigborough, a chapel
of ease was built at Salcott Wigborough for the
villagers: it was served by the vicar of Great
Wigborough.

In 1317 Salcott was recorded as being a market
town, with paved streets and, later, in 1372 its people
decided they should have their own rector. They put
in a request to the Bishop of London, in whose
diocese Essex then was. A commission was set up,
depositions made, but no change seems to have taken
place. Salcott remained a chapel to Great Wigborough
until the 19th century.

In 1480 a chantry was formed in the church by
John Baron, with a Chantry Priest to sing and
administer the Holy Sacraments. All this was dissolved
about 1550 and the church plate was confiscated and
the chantry lands given to John Raynforth – who also
stole the church bells. At that period there were 140
'Houseling people' [Communicants].

The Salcott church of St Mary stands at the
western end of Salcott Street, with the creek quite
close behind it. Constructed of flint, rubble and
septaria, with a dressing of limestone, it consists of a
chancel, nave and south porch of the early 16th
century, with blocks of stone carefully restored and
with a gable of flint panelling. The roofs are tiled
and there is a 15th century west tower of embattled
knapped flint in the perpendicular style. The tower
holds one bell inscribed Pack and Chapman of London,

1771. The church was much restored in 1892/3 at a cost of £1,446.

Salcott should be visited in the spring, when the wild snowdrops grow in the rambling churchyard overlooking open farmland and the Salcott Marshes. There is a beautiful twofold south door of the early 16th century and an unusual chair of the 17th century with a high panelled back in the chancel. The pulpit is hexagonal with raised inlay panels, dating from the 18th century. The east window has three fine stained-glass panels of Jesus, St Helena and St Cedd, in memory of the Smith family (1886-1928).

Two distinguished figures in Salcott in the 16th century were the Capon brothers, John and William, who must often have worshipped in this church. They were associated with the dramatic quarrel of Henry VIII and the Pope, which changed English history. The brothers went to Cambridge University and were friends of Cardinal Wolsey. William was his chaplain and was appointed dean of the famous college at Ipswich, established by Wolsey. He was later Master of Jesus College, Cambridge, until four years before his death in 1550. John rose to even higher position and was abbot of St Benet's Abbey in Norfolk. In 1529 he journeyed to Cambridge to persuade William and other dignitaries to declare in favour of the King's divorce from Catherine of Aragon. His reward for success was appointment as Abbot of Hyde, near Winchester, and his name was among those who actually wrote to Pope Clement VII begging him to consent to the divorce. A year later Henry wrote himself, asking the Pope to allow the Archbishop of Canterbury and the Abbots of Westminster and Hyde to pass judgement on the matter.

Two years later Henry nominated John Capon to the Bishopric of Bangor in North Wales. He was consecrated Bishop by Archbishop Thomas Cranmer, despite the Pope's disapproval. In his new office he was known as John Salcot. A few years later, when

the monasteries were being suppressed, he willingly –
or, at least, wisely – gave Hyde Abbey to the King,
who made him Bishop of Salisbury, the post he held
until his death in 1557.

Baring-Gould's description of Salcott was 'a
small village of old cottages', though the church with
its handsome tower of flints 'has been rather too
vigorously restored'.

The main population groups at Salcott across
the wooden bridge and consisted of labourers and men
more or less engaged in the contraband trade. Every
house had its shed and its stable, where there was a
donkey and cart to be let, on occasions, to smuggle
goods inland.

The ruined church of St Mary's, Virley, stands
in the Old Rectory grounds. It was declared unsafe in
1879, when the last service was held there: however,
the declaration of redundancy of the building was not
declared until November, 1975.

In Baring-Gould's day it was 'a small hunch-
backed edifice in the last stages of delapidation, in a
graveyard unhedged, unwalled'. The church was of
timber and brick, put up anyhow on older stone
foundations and warped and cracked. It was scrambled
over with ivy. The lattice windows were bulged in by
the violence of past storms and the bellcot leant on
one side like a drunkard. Near this decayed church is
a gabled farm and this and a cottage form Virley
village.

Baring-Gould's amusing description of Virley
church is worth reprinting further. He described it as
'Not bigger than a stable that consists of two stalls
and a loose box, whereof the loose box represents the
chancel'.

When the curate in charge preached from the
pulpit he was able to cuff the boys in the west
gallery who 'whispered, cracked nuts or snored'.

'The bellringer stood in the gallery and had
much ado to guard his knuckles from abrasions at

each upcast of the bell-rope; when the movement was double quick for a wedding, like Mehalah's, his knuckles came continually in contact with the plaster and when they did an oath was audible throughout the sacred building between the clangours of the bells.

'The altar possessed no cover, save the curate's red cotton handkerchief, a box contained the much battered communion plate, an iron-moulded surplice with high collar, a register-book the pages glued together with damp and a brush and pan.

'The communion rails had rotted at the bottom and when there was a communion service the clerk cautioned the kneelers not to lean against the balustrade, lest they should be precipitated upon the sanctuary floor.'

Today St Mary's is still a wild-flower-covered ruin, but in the remains of the building where the strange wedding of Mehalah and Rebow took place, both chancel and nave can still be distinguished.

Baring-Gould once said that the congregation consisted largely of local smugglers who attended, not to pay homage to God, but to keep an eye on their contraband goods hidden in various parts of the church.

Near the church was the former 'White Hart' smuggling inn, now replaced by modern houses.

Looking at Salcott and Virley from the creek one can imagine the villagers engaged in the contraband trade more than a century ago. The donkey carts probably carried smuggled goods inland to Tiptree Heath, used as a clearing house by Essex smugglers. The booty was concealed in underground chambers cunningly concealed by vegetation and remained there until it was distributed to further flung locations.

You can still enjoy a pint in the Sun Inn, Salcott, which is built on the site of the historic inn where Mehalah sought employment after fleeing the ardent attentions of Rebow. But the landlady was rude to her and told the poor girl to go back to her future bridegroom - who she did not really want to marry.

There is a local story that one night the men of Salcott were taken by surprise! For a change they were sleeping peacefully in their beds when a boat stole stealthily up the creek and a gang of men landed near the church. Entering the holy place they ascended the tower, removed the bells and bore them off to Holland.

Kipling's "A Smuggler's Song" could have been written with Salcott cum Virley in mind:

Five and twenty ponies
Trotting through the dark
Brandy for the Parson,
'Baccy for the Clerk,
Laces for a lady, letters for a spy,
Watch the wall, my darling, while the Gentlemen go by!

Salcott is mentioned in F G Emmison's *Eliza bethan life in the wills of Essex gentry and yeomen*.

"John Brett of Tolleshunt Major, Essex, yeoman 14 July 1572. To widow Creake her dwelling in the parsonage of Tolleshunt Major for life, if my lease so long continue, without rent. To the poor of Gold-hanger 20s. and Little Totham 20s. To the poor of Tollesbury 6s.8d, Great Tey 10s., Earl's Colne 10s. and Salcott 13s.4d."

Another John Brett, yeoman of Tollesbury, in 1593 seems a very Christian and caring man:

"To the parish of St Botolph in Colchester 40s. to be paid to the Collectors for the poor to be laid out yearly forever, for wood by their discretion, to be sold to those that have most need at 1d. the cubit. To the poor of Salcott 10s., Tolleshunt Major 6s.8d., Tollesbury 10s., Goldhanger 6s.8d. To the prisoners in Colchester Castle 13s.4d. in bread and beer at sundry times. To the Godly preacher to make a sermon to them at the time of distribution 5d."

John Whyte, alias Cowper, living in Coggeshall
was a weaver and clothmaker. In 1558 he left to
Richard Whyte of Salcott "20s. and one of my best
coats, a good doublet and a good pair of hoses, a
new shirt, a petticoat, a cap and my best shoon.
"At my burial there be bestowed in mass and
dirige by note with other charitable deeds to the poor
26s.8d. There be said a low dirige with mass to the
sum of 6s.8d. At my twelve month day a high mass
and dirige to 6s.8d."

In Elizabethan times - and, indeed, much
earlier - the courts of law were very complicated.
The Lord of the Manor had the power to hold his
own court, as did the church; so the people walked a
tricky tightrope between the two great powers. After
the Reformation and the expulsion of the Catholic
Church from England, the Church of England still
perpetuated these ecclesiastical courts. Salcott and
Virley came under the jurisdiction of Colchester. The
Archdeacon would appoint a judge and permanent
officers, like the registrar and, having no headquarters, courts were held at three-weekly intervals
in halls, inns and any other available rooms.

The Archdeacon's annual visitation courts
around Easter and synods about Michaelmas were
attended compulsorily by the clergy, churchwardens
and sidesmen: these could be held at the Archdeacon's own residence.

Millers were proverbially dishonest and Edward
Man, the miller of Fingringhoe, was charged with
seducing a wench in Salcott Mill, where the girl then
lived with her master, Robert Mavis.

There was a Salcott man involved in a church
court slander case in 1571: Robert Long said that
ministers' wives were whores and their children
bastards. For this he was given public penance 'to
stand two Saturdays following, with a paper upon his
head in Colchester Market, and there openly
acknowledge his fault and the like in the parish

church of Salcott the next two Sundays'.

Parish officers sometimes blotted their copy-book: one defendant was Thomas Minkes, Warden of Salcott church, who in 1593 'carried away the wine from the minister which was left at the communion'.

There was some clerical drunkenness in 1588: W Orwin, rector of Fryerning, was 'an alehouse keeper' and Mr Roberts, late curate of Salcott, was called 'a tosspot, alehouse haunter and table-player'.

Little Virley had its own scandals for Richard Mott was charged in 1590 of marrying his wife's sister. He stated that about 16 years before he married Margaret Graunte, with whom he lived for 5 years until she died, so he married Elizabeth Gaunte, her sister, by whom he had divers children.

By 1923 the Rev F W Bussell was Lord of the Manor in Virley. The Post Office was in Salcott, but money orders and the telegraph office was two miles further away at Tolleshunt D'Arcy. Letters were delivered via Witham.

The Free School was at Salcott and the vicar for the twin parishes was Rev F Crate.

Fred Bacon had the romantic-sounding Love-downs Farm: Clifford Downes was the village black-smith; and Mrs P Foakes was behind the bar at Virley's White Hart Inn. Vince Hall Farm was tilled by William Mann and his sons, while James Ponder had Paynes Farm. The Post Office was managed by Bertie Back as sub-postmaster. The mixed elementary school, which had been built in 1870, had, in 1923, 70 pupils under the headmistress-ship of Mrs Jackson. Salcott's Rising Sun was managed by E Beecham and the local coal dealer, pork butcher and shopkeeper were Elijah Foakes, John Ponder and Harry Foakes respectively.

The total population of the villages was 274, living on 346 acres of land, of which 150 was farmed.

ST. MARY – SALCOTT.